George Nowitzky

Norfolk, the Marine Metropolis of Virginia and the Sound and River Cities of North Carolina

A Narrative

George Nowitzky

Norfolk, the Marine Metropolis of Virginia and the Sound and River Cities of North Carolina
A Narrative

ISBN/EAN: 9783744775502

Printed in Europe, USA, Canada, Australia, Japan

Cover: Foto ©Thomas Meinert / pixelio.de

More available books at **www.hansebooks.com**

THE

Marine Metropolis of Virginia,

AND THE

SOUND AND RIVER CITIES OF NORTH CAROLINA.

A NARRATIVE

BY

GEO. I. NOWITZKY.

NORFOLK, VA., AND RALEIGH, N. C.:
PUBLISHED BY GEO. I. NOWITZKY.
1888.

Entered, according to Act of Congress, in the year 1887, by
GEO. I. NOWITZKY,
In the Office of the Librarian of Congress, at Washington, D. C.

PRESSES OF
E. M. UZZELL,
RALEIGH, N. C.

PREFACE.

In writing this book I have endeavored to comply with the following rules:

FIRST. In describing places of interest and noted or public buildings, to write of them only as they exist. It is true that some buildings devoted to business, on account of striking architectural features, had to be described, and, as a consequence, are described; but I guarantee that none of the misleading puffery will be found in this little effort which, unfortunately, accompany many of the guides to other cities, and makes them a source of ridicule in place of desired information.

SECOND. In writing up historical events, to narrate them as they occurred, using only facts gleaned from indisputed authority.

THIRD. Not to permit the promise of reward, in the form of advertising patronage, to control or in any way interfere with my views or descriptions. This accounts for the absence of a number of advertisements which are usually loudest in other publications. No puffs were promised; in fact, it was stipulated that none must be expected.

And last, not to solicit any advertisements from the designers of any of the

BUILDINGS DESCRIBED.

This is the reason that Norfolk's worthy representatives of a profession whose great service to mankind can be traced back further than medicine or the law are not to be found in the professional directory; and *I can further solemnly assert that I am not* acquainted with an architect in Norfolk, or have ever spoken to one, to my knowledge. I make this statement to show that I was not prejudiced in favor of any of them; and, as a consequence, my descriptions are entirely impartial, my object being to draw a picture that the people of Norfolk could look upon and say: "This is a sketch of our city as seen by an impartial stranger"; and the stranger, after using it as a guide, takes it to his home as a souvenir, realizing that it is a description of Norfolk as it is.

Having thus given the rules which guided my descriptions, I respectfully call the attention of the reader to the following

EXPLANATIONS,

which bring this rather long preface to a conclusion:

Extensive travel in most of the lustrous combination of States and Territories which form our common country has taught me that the way to improve a city is not by favorably exaggerating the appearance of her architectural and other improvements, but by pointing out objectionable defects as well as gratifying effects. Experience, gained the same way, has also taught me that the majority of people, in reading descriptions of their cities, prefer flattery to facts. I write this because I fear that some of the citizens of Norfolk, upon a hasty perusal of this work, may think that I have been unnecessarily sarcastic at the expense of some of their buildings; but I am satisfied all this will be dispelled when they deliberate and realize that flattery blocks all roads to improvement, while an honest narration, even if it verges on sarcasm, acts as a spur, and often forces us on the direct road to an excelling point. Other buildings will have to be built, and the only way we can improve is by not shutting our eyes to glaring faults in existing structures.

PREFACE.

I can further say, that in all the vast territory which lies between the Canadian boundary and the Mexican line I have never found, in city, town or village, a community whose cordial greeting was more sincere and whose arms of honest hospitality have been wider open to me. For these reasons, I can conscientiously write that my pen has been guided by a mind entirely free from prejudice, and possessing only the kindest feelings towards Norfolk and her people. If it has displeased even the most fastidious, I hope they will realize—

>That if I've sinned,
>   I've sinned without design;
>To sin is innate in all,
>   "To forgive is divine."

GEO. I. NOWITZKY.

NORFOLK, VA., Nov. 18, 1887.

NORFOLK;

THE

Marine Metropolis of Virginia.

A NARRATIVE.

CHAPTER I.

WHICH SHOWS THE STRONG RELATIONSHIP EXISTING EVERY DAY SUNDAY EXCEPTED, BETWEEN PORTSMOUTH, VIRGINIA, AND SIX-TEN P. M.—DESCRIBES NORFOLK HARBOR. AND GIVES A PICTURE IN TYPE OF THE CITY OF NORFOLK AS SEEN FROM THE OPPOSITE SHORE.

It was six-ten P. M. in Portsmouth, Virginia, and all the good citizens of Portsmouth, Virginia, knew it. I say all unhesitatingly. The deaf and dumb knew it, for the train of the Seaboard road, bringing in the Tar-Heel mail, traverses the entire breadth of the city through its leading business avenue, High street, and as a consequence is so conspicuous that they could not help but see it. The blind also had no reasonable excuse for not knowing that it was six-ten P. M., for the movement was accompanied by such shrill whistles at every street crossing, and the ceaseless ringing of the enterprising locomotive bell, that no reasonable blind man could help but hear it; and as the few blind people that grope their way through the streets of Portsmouth are as reasonable and as far-seeing as blind people are anywhere, I can safely assert that even they knew it was that hour; for, for so many years have the "management" of the Seaboard road scheduled and advertised that time, as the time of the arrival of that train, that the citizens of Portsmouth accept it as a fact that six-ten P. M. and the train make their appearance simultaneously every day, except Sunday, when restless Time still jogs ahead, and the train, as if to give Portsmouth watches and clocks an opportunity to prove themselves indispensable, takes a rest.

It had been a dark, a very dark and very cloudy day, accompanied by a very high wind, and at every one of the numerous stations at which we stopped "new passenger," before entering the car, had wisely looked at the sky and as wisely predicted a cyclone that would blow the train off the track, or a flood that, by washing away the bridges, would prove equally disastrous and fully as dangerous to life.

About the time every passenger not himself endowed with prophetic judgment was getting tired of these doleful predictions the weather came to our relief with a complete change; for the wind lulled, and a dismal, disagreeable rain commenced, accompanied with such unseasonable crashes of thunder and vivid darts and flashes of lightning, which appeared to be diverted only by a miracle from striking the train, that the wisest passengers immediately thought that it was necessary for the most nervous to glean the information (in spite of statistical contradiction) that the chances of a train in motion being struck by lightning was greater than any other moving body or stationary spot on earth.

This inspiring weather and assuring conversation continued without intermission until six-ten, and Portsmouth came to our relief like a pair of soothing angels.

Nothing cheers the average traveler more and puts him in better spirits than, after riding all day through rain and darkness, to find everything that looks forbidding and threatening gradually breaking away in favor of light and sunshine. As for myself, when I left the train, feeling exceedingly buoyant and refreshed by the unmistakable signs of fair weather which could be seen at nearly every cardinal point, I took a long, lingering look at Portsmouth, with the sun bravely struggling to dispel the dark clouds in order to set clear, and then walked down to the ferry, which had just arrived, and in a few seconds found myself standing on the end pointed towards

NORFOLK HARBOR.

Here a scene of marine activity and picturesque blending of sky, land, water, naval architecture (embracing everything at the present time afloat, with the probable exception of a Chinese junk and the piratical-looking Algerine fishing smack) and land architecture as varied and remarkable as can be seen in the same space anywhere upon the globe.

For fear that the critical reader may judge hastily, and think that I am overdrawing, I repeat—varied and remarkable. I'll readily admit that there are many other cities, both foreign and domestic, that show more heroic architecture. It is true she has no mosque of St. Sophia, accompanied by many tapering minarets to break the sky-line, like the great city of the Bosphorus—Constantinople; nor those great eye-centres, St. Paul's Cathedral and the Victoria Tower, the prominent elevations of Britain's (or rather, the world's) metropolis—London; nor a gilded dome to crown a high hill, like Massachusetts' capital city—Boston; or a natural feature (the smoking mountain, Vesuvius) which has made famous Naples and her matchless bay. But Norfolk harbor has many surroundings peculiar to herself and entirely unlike these or any other port.

To my immediate right I observed the huge warehouses and substantial wharves of the Seaboard road; tied to the latter were a number of schooners and the palatial bay steamer Virginia, keeping time, with a gentle up-and-down motion, to the ceaseless movement of the restless tide. To the left were a number of three-masted ice schooners (and one with four masts), discharging their frozen cargo, as well as a number of large foreign iron steam-ships, flying Spanish, English and Norwegian colors, and all swayed by the same lazy but never-failing motion. Further to the right, standing in bold relief, were the bright, yellow-painted buildings of the Navy Yard, backed by the distant green woods (a pleasing contrast) which look as if they were the boundary of that part of the harbor. The formidable receiving-ship Franklin, floating as gracefully as if she were a huge swan, next attracted my attention.

Directly opposite the part described is the busy waterfront of bustling

BERKLEY,

teeming with cumbersome-looking derricks, ways, marine railways, railroads, wharves (continually strained by the weight of heavily-loaded freight cars), and back of them green trees, private residences, saw-mills, the old abandoned Marine Hospital, huge lumber piles, freight sheds, etc., all in such a magnificent but pleasing confusion that one cannot help but think that they had once occupied different localities, but had, in some unaccountable way, drifted together; and that the tall, grim-looking escapes of the mammoth lumber-driers, which tower above all surroundings, were placed there as sentinels to keep them from scattering and once again occupying their former sites; this confusion, however, is pleasing to the eye, and makes the harbor all the more picturesque. But directly in the immediate front were the two crowning beauties, which, more than all else, fixed the restless eye. The first was the superb stretch of water, carrying upon its mirrored surface a magnificent moving panorama, among which I noticed the black hulk and light upper works of the powerful "Cape Charles," loaded with passengers comfortably seated in the palatial cars which were to carry them by land to New York, after transporting them safely through miles of Chesapeake's white-capped waves; fretful, busy tugs, which, as if not content by displacing water themselves, were towing monster barges with timbers groaning under the weight of cargo; great ocean ships, their decks covered with weary crew, with eyes thankfully lingering upon the hospitable shore-lines of this favored part of the Old Dominion; trim, brightly-painted river steam-boats, filled with joyous passengers; a heavier but just as daintily decorated steamer, evidently intended for bay passenger business; and last, a fussy little launch from the Navy Yard, which looked and acted as if alive, and knew that the only way it could attract attention among these larger surroundings was by making as much noise as possible. But the eye could not linger here long, for back of all this pleasing combination of floating life and business stood

THE CITY OF NORFOLK,

her buildings so densely massed that I could scarcely trace a single street, and having such a uniform and compact appearance as to give the impression that the whole had been designed by some master architect, moulded by superior mechanics and securely placed upon the most appropriate spot—its present site. Her substantial-looking wharves, fringed with the tall masts of stately ships and the smoke-stacks of fleet steamers; further back the solid walls of the warehouses and stores that line her water-front; and above them all a grand display of spires, towers, pinnacles and domes.

CHAPTER II.

WHICH, LIKE THE PRECEDING ONE, MAY BE CRITICISED AS BEING INCONSISTENT, ON ACCOUNT OF DESCRIBING THINGS THAT ARE FOREIGN TO THE SUBJECT, BUT UPON REFLECTION WILL BE FOUND INDISPENSABLE—IT CONTINUES THE DESCRIPTION OF ONE OF THOSE SOUTHERN SUNSETS FOR WHICH NORFOLK IS SO FAMOUS, AS WELL AS HER GREATEST FEATURE, HER MAGNIFICENT HARBOR—THEN DELVES SUFFICIENTLY INTO HISTORY TO SHOW THAT NORFOK GAINED NOTHING BY THE VISIT OF TOM MOORE—AND CONCLUDES WITH THE AUTHOR'S REASONS FOR GIVING THESE PAGES TO THE PUBLIC.

It looked as if Nature's "boss painter" was conscious of the fact that he had the opportunity of making his work the attraction of the evening, and for this reason was exceedingly lavish with his coloring materials, particularly the two extremes—somber, funeral black and the brightest shining gold, and as if to show that he had exclusive control and could do as he pleased, he reversed the usual order of things and threw most of his fire and gilding to the north-east.

A mass of burnished gold appeared as a background to the tower of the Baptist church and made its numerous pinnacles stand out in unusually bold relief, while a generous daub of the same material back of the courthouse gave the dome of that judicial structure a prominence and dignity worthy of the honorable courts that are housed in the main structure.

Further to the right the tall steeple of the Central Presbyterian church, surrounded by a fainter glow, looked graceful as well as solid, and the many feet of spire which reaches the sky above St. Mary's had as a background a fleecy white cloud which looked as if silver and ivory had flown together and, thoroughly blending, had formed a color for the special purpose of confusing artists.

This remarkable blending of sky, earth and water, this peaceful harmony of the natural and artificial, forced my mind into a reverie—caused me to muse, and as I continued to look at the city, her towers, dome and spires bathed in golden sunshine and silvery fleece, I could not help but ask myself if this could possibly be the same Norfolk so much abused and slandered by

TOM MOORE,

who evidently thought that the only way he could pay for his passage across the ocean (in the sloop-of-war "built of Bermuda cedar") and cancel other English obligations was by abusing America, Americans and all foreign writers who had a good word for either.

The first American soil pressed by this "sweetest of singers" was that which acts as a site for the city of Norfolk, and it was in 1804, just after a terrible epidemic had visited the city, and many citizens were in mourning for the loss of relatives and friends who had been stricken by the death-dealing fever.

But venom in place of sugar fell from the lips of the great bard; in place of a tear for the dead and a word of sympathy for the living, this remarkable writer, who could make his pen weep over the fate of some mythological heroine, or an imaginary hero who, with mind unhinged, was presumed to wander through the neighboring Dismal Swamp in search of an equally imaginary maiden, abused Norfolk and Virginia hospitality in their darkest hour with the following lines:

"Norfolk, it must be owned, presents an unfavorable specimen of America. The characteristics of Virginia in general are not such as can delight either the politician or the moralist, and at Norfolk they are exhibited in their least attractive form. At the time when we arrived the yellow fever had not yet disappeared, and every odor that assailed us in the streets very strongly accounted for its visitation."

When a man at first recalls these words, he may be for the moment prejudiced against this city, but his prejudice will melt like butter in a refiner's furnace when memory glides back and refreshes itself with the undeniable fact that this same Tom Moore jeeringly described the government and citizens of the United States by the following uncomplimentary and undeserved couplets:

"Already in this free, this virtuous state,
Which, Frenchmen tell us, was ordained by fate
To show the world what high perfection springs
From rabble senators and merchant kings—
Even here already, patriots learn to steal
Their private perquisites from public weal;
And guardians of the country's sacred fire,
Like Afric's priests, let out the flame for hire;—
Those vaunted demagogues, who nobly rose
From England's debtors to be England's foes,
Who could their monarch in their purse forget,
And break allegiance but to cancel debt."

* * * * * * * * *

"Oh! Freedom, Freedom, how I hate thy cant!
Not Eastern bombast, not the savage rant

Of purpled madmen, were they numbered all,
From Roman Nero down to Russian Paul,
Could grate upon my ear so mean, so base,
As the rank jargon of that factious race,
Who, poor of heart and prodigal of words,
Formed to be slaves, yet struggling to be lords."

That the same Tom Moore, who, not being himself endowed with sufficient prophetic judgment to realize that the then small, scattered village of Washington would be bound, with the increase of the nation's population and wealth, to become (as it has) a great city, sneers thus at the patriot of that date who dared to make the prediction:

"In fancy now, beneath the twilight gloom,
Come let me lead thee o'er this 'second Rome,'
Where tribunes rule, where dusky Davi bow,
And what was Goose Creek once is Tiber now;—
This embryo capital, where Fancy sees
Squares in morasses, obelisks in trees;
Which second-sighted seers even now adorn
With shrines unbuilt and heroes yet unborn."

And that this same Tom Moore, Irish by birth but unlike the majority of Erin's sons, was so thoroughly wedded to the English aristocracy and dyed in English prejudices that everything American was so obnoxious that he could forget himself sufficiently to describe the "Father of his Country," Washington, who is generally conceded by all nations as among the purest of statesmen and the peer of any man that the world has ever produced, with these ill-chosen words:

"But hold!—observe yon little mount of pines,
Where the breeze murmurs and the fire-fly shines.
There let thy fancy raise, in bold relief,
The sculptured image of that veteran chief
Who lost the rebel's in the hero's name,
And climbed o'er prostrate loyalty to fame;
Beneath whose sword Columbia's patriot train
Cast off their monarch, that their mob might reign.
How shall we rank thee upon glory's page?
Thou more than soldier and just less than sage!
Of peace too fond to act the conqueror's part,
Too long in camps to learn a statesman's art."

As I was thus studying the man and his literary works, the engineer's bell was tapped by the pilot in the wheel-house, and as the boat glided out of her slip I dismissed from my mind, for the time being, this "great poet," who had enriched the world's libraries with "Lalla Rookh" as well as the libellous American letters (not, however, until I had concluded that I had considerable admiration for the genius of the poet and fully as much contempt for Tom Moore as a man), and once again took a glance at my surroundings as we sailed out 'midst the golden sunshine.

Every revolution of the wheel, every foot of headway, revealed new beauties as our boat plowed through the shimmering, glistening water, which looked like the realization of a day-dream. Near midstream one of the huge sea-going barges of the Cape Charles line, loaded with two heavy freight trains, was slowly being dragged by two powerful tugs towards the "Roads," closely followed by one of the Chesapeake and Albemarle Canal Company's boats, which had in tow a literal procession of small craft which had just left the placid waters of that great canal. As this remarkable floating variety was directly in our course, our captain prudently brought our boat to a halt. This gave us an excellent opportunity to view the harbor from a central standpoint.

To the west, the dense bank of shrubbery and trees of the Marine Park, back of the Naval Hospital, looked like a solid green wall, and, crowned by the fire of the setting sun, made a most impressive contrast of colors. A little further to the north we had a good view of the deep waterway which connects the harbor with the "Roads," the bay and the ocean. Almost due north, a little west, Lambert's Point, with its gigantic trestle projecting far into the water, looked like a piece of delicate lace held from the sky by some mysterious magician with invisible threads; while the bridge of the Norfolk and Western road, crossing the Eastern Branch just a little south of east, looked fully as picturesque as the celebrated wharf at Lambert's, and appeared as if it had been placed there for no other purpose than to complete the picture.

As I was contemplating this scene, which, in spite of the fact that it was not the first time that I had crossed the Elizabeth, still had many attractions for me, several gentlemen, whom I had met before while traveling, came to where I was standing; and one of them, who is known as a man that has traveled extensively in Europe as well as America, and is considered a walking encyclopædia appertaining to the sights of all the larger cities of the United States and the British Isles, addressed the following words to me:

"I hope this blockade will not delay us long enough for us to miss the Baltimore boat, for I certainly would hate to be forced to lay over in Norfolk for twenty-four hours."

"It is our own fault," interrupted one of his companions, "for we should have taken the boat when we first got off the train, in place of taking chances by coming over here; besides, it's very likely the two merchants we want to see will be at supper when we pass their stores, so there will be nothing gained. But you can rest assured that if I lose the boat I shall go to Baltimore on the first train, even if I have to lose the Bay-Line part of my ticket. No twenty-four hours for me in Norfolk!"

"Why is it," I asked, "that you have such an aversion for Norfolk? I have never heard of travelers being mistreated there; in fact, the people enjoy the reputation of being exceedingly hospitable."

"There are good people everywhere," replied the last speaker, "and Norfolk is no exception. I am satisfied that she has as hospitable a class of inhabitants as any other city; but if all a man wants is to find good citizens, my advice to him is to stay at home and save his money: he can find them there. As for myself, my traveling business forces me to see stores and store-windows every day, and if there is anything more attractive about the make-up of the city than the plate-glass of Main street, I don't know it. As a consequence, when

I have a few days off, I prefer to go to a city that has parks, libraries, art galleries, monuments and heroic architecture."

"Every word true," remarked the first speaker, solemnly shaking his head and looking very grave, his eyes fixed upon mine as he continued: "Norfolk, my friend, has a population composed of most excellent citizens, I also happily admit; but that she is burdened with parks or places of sufficient interest to pay the traveler to lay over to see, I certainly deny. Why, sir, although I have been there at least ten times, I can solemnly assert that I have never been outside of Market Square and Main street."

"Probably the reason that you have never found anything there to interest you can easily be accounted for by what you've just admitted—that is, that you have limited your explorations to those two streets."

"Now, my friend," replied the gentleman with much American and some European experience, "if you are trying to convince us that Norfolk has any overlooked attractions, you might as well quit, for you are wasting sweetness. Where are her parks, her boulevards, her art galleries, her churches and assembly halls that are world-famed for faultless design or grand appearance, and last, the public monuments to her great dead? Tom Moore, when he came here years ago, found nothing in Norfolk that he thought was worth describing, and nothing has been erected since; he actually had to go into the very heart of the Dismal Swamp to find something to write about, and ——"

My friend's remarks came to an abrupt termination on account of the boat making her slip, and, in his hurry to make the Baltimore boat, he got so far ahead of me that we became separated, and the conversation was never resumed. But although my friends were not with me, I could not help pondering over their remarks. I had been in Norfolk before, and only knew her to love her; but I had to admit that much of what they said was, unfortunately, true. My memory could not recall any great park or parkway within its limits; and as for monuments and statues, although Norfolk has produced many men that deserve them—where are they? Where is the statue to her greatest soldier, mighty Pickett, who lived and died within her limits, and who led, in July, 1863, one of the greatest charges that history has indellibly placed upon her pages? And where is the towering monument that should be the most conspicuous of her elevations, to commemorate the deeds of the men of Norfolk, who, under his command, braved death a hundred times as they charged into the midst of destruction, into the very centre of death—"Bloody Angle"? And the Norfolk sailors who, with Buchanan, in March, 1862, on the Virginia or Merrimac, sent the Cumberland to the bottom of Hampton Roads, burned the Congress, and forced the Monitor to retreat? And also the heroes on Craney Island, who forced proud Admiral Cockburn to withdraw his British fleet in 1813, and thus saved the city?

As they have not been erected, I naturally concluded that the citizens of Norfolk must have labored under the erroneous impression that their connection with great achievements will save their names from "sinking into oblivion." I say erroneous impression, because, in passing, in a passenger steamer, almost over the same course taken by the contending iron-clads in the celebrated battle of the Roads, which caused a complete revolution in combative marine construction, out of over sixty passengers of over average intelligence, only three could tell the name of the commander of the ram Virginia.

But that Norfolk had nothing worth seeing no argument could force my mind to believe, so satisfied was I that a city situated upon a site which was purchased two hundred and five years back on account of the great advantages it possessed as a shipping point; was immediately made a trade centre, and protected by laws not enjoyed by any colony of that date; was first incorporated by Royal Charter in 1736, and, although named a borough, enjoyed everything that appertained to the machinery of a city—a mayor, board of aldermen and police, and in 1845 was made a city in fact by the General Assembly of the State of Virginia; is situated upon one of the finest harbors in the world; and last and best of all, has been blest from the first by an industrious and intelligent population;—that population certainly has left its impress in the form of engineering, landscape and architectural features worthy of more than passing notice. To discover these I concluded to make it my mission, and immediately prepared to start on a voyage of discovery—to penetrate and explore that vast tract of avenues, streets and lanes faced by stone, brick and iron, which lies north of the great length of Main street, and is as little known to the majority of travelers as the untrodden centre of Australia or the unknown depths of burning Orizaba, and if I was successful in finding the interesting features which I was quite certain existed, to write a book, in which I would give the traveling public the benefit of my observations, and make it, if possible, sufficiently interesting and readable to be worthy of perusal by the resident population.

CHAPTER III.

WHICH DESCRIBES MAIN STREET—THE ROOFLESS APPEARANCE OF THE HARE BUILDING AND THE MUCH-ROOFED ATLANTIC HOTEL—THE WHITE MARBLE COTTON EXCHANGE AND THE GRANITE GOVERNMENT BUILDING—THE ST. JAMES—YOUNG MEN'S CHRISTIAN ASSOCIATION BUILDING—THE ACADEMY OF MUSIC—DEPOTS, ETC.

Main street being the great retail shopping avenue of the city, and as it contains the most costly buildings, I concluded to make it the subject of my first street sketch, although subsequent discoveries showed me that there is a street in Norfolk which by far eclipses it in the possession of points of interest to the stranger, and in variety is second to none in the South.

Main street begins at a combination of the busiest, cleanest, best constructed, and least obstructed by unsightly sheds of any of the leading wharves of this active port, for I found no buildings to block the range of my eyes as they feasted upon the wealth of green trees and shrubbery of the opposite shore, and my immediate surroundings were sufficiently mixed to interest the most fastidious.

As I faced the noble expanse of water, I found to the left the great shed of the Baltimore Steam Packet Company, which, during business hours, has a continual stream of glossy carriages, many hued omnibuses, heavy drays, trucks, express wagons, etc., entering or leaving its capacious doorway, which looked as if it might make an appropriate entrance to the Mammoth Cave of Kentucky. After a glance to the right at the heavy ships of the Boston line and a number of huge ocean steam tramps receiving cargo, I faced about, and my attention was immediately attracted by the grim-looking tower of the Virginia Compress, which showed plainly what it was intended for, not only by the white clouds of escaping steam and the deafening noise that accompanied them, but also by the many bales of cotton that would find their way into its somber-looking interior large and clumsy and leave reduced to less than half their former size, in order to take up less space in a ship's hold while in transit across Atlantic's stormy space to Liverpool and other European ports, or up the coast to New England factories, part to be shipped back in a short time manufactured into many different fabrics, in order to give the citizens of Norfolk and the cotton-raisers of the contiguous section the proud privilege of paying several times its original cost, the difference, except a very slight margin, finding its way into the strong safes of the owners of the "foreign bottoms" which move it both ways and the distant manufacturers that weave it into cloth. That cotton factories should be erected here, and that they should be filled with thousands of skilled employés to weave this raw product into profitable fabrics, not one of the citizens of Norfolk will deny; but, unfortunately, she is not true to her best interest in this respect, for in my rambles through the city my ears failed to catch the cheery music that accompanies the rapid whirl of the spindles.

From here onward the street is utilized for the display of a majority of the best office, commercial and hotel buildings in the city; and I can say without hesitancy, after a careful study of the miles of varied facades which line this noble thoroughfare, that they will compare favorably with those of any city of its size on the Atlantic seaboard.

The first building I passed that attracted my attention is the late creation known as the

HARE BUILDING,

which, with its abbreviated cornice, roofless appearance, but excellent display of terra-cotta, is, in many ways, one of the most remarkable studies in the city—remarkable from the fact that it is unlike any other within its limits. The upper floors are cut up for offices, and are well adapted for the purpose. This is particularly appreciated by the cotton people, as quite a number are occupied by them. As I looked at this building, which forces the impression that something is lacking, and that something the roof, which appears to have departed with part of the cornice, my eyes wandered about the street, evidently for the purpose of discovering the missing and necessary house-covering. I did not have to strain my optics, for as soon as they rested on the building nearly opposite (just a little to the left), I scarcely could refrain from startling the pedestrians who were walking up and down the side-walk by exclaiming "Eureka!" for there, standing in bold relief, I found the

ATLANTIC HOTEL,

the greatest possible contrast to the building just described, for it appeared at a first glance to be all roof, and imagination could easily shape itself so as to believe that the double-decked mansard of the north-east corner is animate, and that its circular upper windows are two eyes longingly gazing at the flat and unfinished-looking Hare building, as if it would like to fly over and take position nearer the earth's surface, using the top of that structure for a base, and thus supplying a very apparent deficiency. As the admiring rustic said of the fat lady when he first beheld that queen of human heavy weight under the frail roof (or rather, weather protection) afforded by the sweeps of a circus canvas, so everybody must say upon beholding the two main fronts of the Atlantic Hotel—"it 's a big thing!" Its front elevations have three streets upon which to display their six hundred and forty feet of attractive brick, slate, iron and glass, for it faces two hundred and fifty feet on Main, two hundred and ten on Granby and one hundred and eighty on Randolph street. The structure is built in what is termed the French chateau style, although I think that an American adaptation of that style would be the proper way of designating it. In France, during the many years that that nation posed as a kingdom or empire, this style was used for what its name indicates—the country palaces or castles of the French nobility; and during these later days of the French Republic, with the exception of an occasional fashionable village inn, surrounded by grounds which afford good opportunities for landscape gardening, it is very seldom used only for the country houses of the aristocracy. In this country our practical fellow-citizens have found a way of adapting it to almost every use from a college building to a furniture factory. In making the designs for the Atlantic, however, the architect has been particularly happy in his treatment of this much-abused type, for he has certainly given it the appearance of solidity, which would have been much heightened if the facings had been of stone instead of wood painted to imitate that material. It has, besides, a cheerful and roomy appearance, and its many large-sized windows give indications of that greatest necessity in hotels—perfect ventilation and natural light. I am satisfied that a glance at this Colossus of brick and slate, from that part of the Post-office side-walk which permits a view of the two main facades, will bring forth the declaration that it is an ornament as well as a landmark of the city.

Opposite this mammoth hotel stands the building which contains the rooms of

THE COTTON EXCHANGE.

It has two more strong claims upon the visiting stranger for inspection. The first is, that it is the only marble building in the city; and the second, that it has the most sensational history of any within its limits, for its white front once graced a street in Baltimore; but it had to be removed to make room for the new post-office building in that city. As a consequence, it was sold, the purchaser being an enterprising Norfolk hotel proprietor, who placed the front on vessels, floated it down the Patapsco and Chesapeake Bay, and then by way of Hampton Roads and Norfolk harbor, and safely landed it upon a wharf near its present site. Its erection here has done much to improve this part of the city, for its white front elevation, topped by a well-designed mansard roof, makes a magnificent contrast to the red glare of the prevailing and rather tiring bricks.

THE GOVERNMENT BUILDING,

in which are housed the Post-office, United States Courts and Custom-house, is next in line. It is a magnificent creation, and without question the finest and costliest building in the city; and, taking into consideration its noble, lofty portico, the faultless design of the entire structure and the enduring nature of the material of which it is built, I am satisfied I will not be contradicted when I declare it the best building in the State of Virginia. It is a classic-looking structure of the Greek type, built of imperishable granite. The solid stone steps, which are of generous width, commence at the street-line, and, after reaching the extreme height of the basement story, terminate at a broad granite platform, upon which stands six massive fluted columns, with Corinthian capitols, which support a triangular pediment with its plain but appropriate tympanum.

Next to this heroic government erection stands the cheerful and hospitable-looking

ST. JAMES HOTEL.

This building was erected in 1879, and known as the Virginian. It was remodeled and one story added in March, 1887. A bad mistake was made in not adding still another, as the foundations, I am credibly informed, are strong enough to bear the additional weight. The popularity of the hotel would have made the room gained profitable, and the additional height would have vastly improved its general appearance. Any one viewing its pressed-brick front from the opposite side-walk can hardly realize that it contains sixty large and elegantly-furnished rooms, besides the ground floor, that contains the cheerful-looking office (which appears to be a rendezvous for merchants and cotton buyers as well as commercial travelers) and the appropriately-decorated dining-room, with its outlook upon busy Main street in front and the refreshing green that surrounds the government building at the side.

Hugging the St. James, in what appears a most Christian-like manner, and overlooking all surroundings, stands the

YOUNG MEN'S CHRISTIAN ASSOCIATION BUILDING.

This promises to be the most showy edifice in the city. Although it is not yet quite completed, the exterior is far enough advanced to warrant the assertion that Main street has received an addition of which the city may well be proud. Nothing appears cramped. The great arch which bears the legend, "Young Men's Christian Association," is a conspicuous feature of the front, as well as the two flanking towers—one a hanging oriel, giving a splendid opportunity for projecting windows; and the other a grand, massive, square, highly-ornamented tower, which overtops all. Everything about the front is rich and consistent. The harmony in the color of the materials employed (brick, stone and terra-cotta) is so thoroughly blended that it will not require time to tone them down, and everything about it shows that it is a study which combines strength, grace, prominence and beauty.

Opposite this array, which stands conspicuous among the best of Norfolk's buildings, will be found the following combination of substantial and well-designed commercial palaces: The stuccoed front and mansard elevation of the Ames & Stevens furniture building; next, the Lowenburg block of fine stores, well built of brick, trimmed with marble, the upper floors nearly all occupied by the legal fraternity. This is followed by the stalwart front of the

ACADEMY OF MUSIC.

The exterior of this building looks decidedly commercial. It is, in fact, a fine business block, containing a large number of stores, and with but little to indicate that it is devoted to the drama. The entrance is, I am sorry to say, disappointing, when compared to either exterior or interior. I never was more surprised in a building in my life than when I walked through the long vestibule and stood in one of the handsomest decorated and most imposing theatres in the South. The auditorium, which has a seating capacity of nearly 1,400, is a work of art throughout. The two circles are rich in relief work; but the crowning glories of this amusement palace are the proscenium and the ceiling. The first is a scholarly blending of emblems appertaining to music and the drama, in semi-relief, entwined in most appropriate scrolls, making an elaborate frame for the boxes as well as the great curtain; the effect, which is very rich, is still further heightened by two angels in full relief, which, with easy pose, sit on the cornice of the top boxes. The ceiling is rich in magnificent frescoes and large medallions, with the busts of dramatic authors and musical composers. The lack of space prevents a further description of this noble interior, of which Norfolk has a just right to be proud.

The Queen Anne facade of the Bank of Commerce, closely followed by the drab stone front of the Norfolk

National Bank, and the solid, fort-like elevation of the granite Marine Bank, on the corner of Bank street, next attracted my attention; then the Burrow and Peter Smith buildings centered the eyes, on account of their conspicuous situation at the head of Market Square. Diagonally across from these last-described trade marts, the ten stores of the Newton building make a graceful curve, and thereby place part of their substantial and business-looking fronts upon Market Square. Next in line I found the solid-looking creation of the

MECHANICS' ASSOCIATION,

which not only indicates by a giant arm clutching a hammer, and appropriately placed in a niche, but also by its general appearance, that the upper story was intended as a hall for public gatherings. From here to Church street both sides of Main have about the same appearance as that usually found on the leading business street of any American city of between thirty and fifty thousand inhabitants, the south side showing the best and most modern structures, particularly those near the corner.

The first building of note, after crossing Church street, is the

PURCELL HOUSE,

which has an airy, pleasing front. This time-honored hotel has quite a history, and it is said that in its long career, under different names, its hospitable roof has given shelter to many foreign as well as native celebrities, among the former the Third Napoleon and Garibaldi. From here on the street throws aside the business-like garb of active trade and attires itself in the less showy garments of private life and buildings fashioned to enjoy it, while stately elms assist in giving it a more retired appearance. Nearly every house is substantially built of brick, with the various kinds of stone facings. All look comfortable, many give evidence of wealth, culture and refinement; but none so remarkably differ in design or detail as to call for special description except two residences. The first stands about midway between Church street and the depot, and which, through a combination of semi-Moorish towers, arches, peculiar windows, stained glass and sculptured embellishments, forces one to believe that it was intended for an art gallery, library or other public use. The other "notable" exception occupies space a little further down on the same side. It is an old brick building, which looks as if it might antedate the Revolution. It has a quaint roof, pierced by dormers, which looks as if it might be the identical house-top that inspired Mansard and gave him the points for his celebrated covering. Its oddity is added to by a bay window which crosses a roadway and is supported in part by the brick wall of the next house.

The street, as I have shown, commences 'midst a scene of active nautical life, and I found that it ends among scenes fully as business-like and by far more noisy, for it appropriately stops near the

PICTURESQUE DEPOT

used by the Norfolk and Western and Norfolk and Southern railroads, with its pretty little park, as well as the Virginia Beach station; in fact, it loses itself among a most remarkable blending of sound and scene— the shrill whistles of the locomotives of three railroad lines; the light, rattling sound of the trains of the Virginia Beach road, as they creep across the trestle towards the ocean; the heavier, rumbling sound of the heavily-loaded freight and passenger trains of the Norfolk and Western and Norfolk and Southern roads, headed· by their locomotives, which seem to strain every energy as they go to and from the depot. It is indeed a most appropriate place for Norfolk's busiest street to find a terminus.

CHAPTER IV.

IN WHICH I WALK THROUGH NORFOLK'S MOST REMARKABLE STREET—STUDY ITS PECULIAR FEATURES—SAY SOMETHING ABOUT ODD FELLOWS' HALL—OLD ST. PAUL'S AND ITS PICTURESQUE GRAVE-YARD—THE PRESBYTERIAN CHURCH, THE HEBREW SYNAGOGUE, THE GREAT HOSPITAL OF ST. VINCENT DE PAUL, AND LESNER'S GARDEN.

Church street is, without any doubt or question, the most remarkable street in the city, if not in the South Atlantic States. There are many streets in the Southern seaboard cities—in fact, too many of them to even attempt an enumeration—that have finer and more costly buildings to grace their fronts, and there are several in this very city of Norfolk that can show a grander architectural display; but no street in this entire combination of States can overshadow Church street in general make-up or variety; and as variety is conceded to be the spice of life, Church street is full of life—all kinds of life. As pure, as honest life as the State of Virginia (so well known for thê purity of her homes) has ever produced can be seen on Church street; and one part of it (fortunately a very small part), shunned by all respectable citizens, is the habitation of the frailest and worst kind of life. Anything obtainable anywhere in this world is supposed to have a duplicate within reach on Church street. If you want the oldest building in the city, go to Church street; if you want the newest, don't leave the street—you can get it: there is always one or more in the process of construction or just finished. The same applies to everything else. If you want the latest imported London-made suit of gent's clothes, or the latest dress made by Worth of Paris, ask for them on Church street; you will not be disappointed, for the facilities of the street are too great to be baffled by three thousand miles of ocean, as it requires, I am credibly informed, only about twelve hours to import from Europe a garment to fit either male or female customer, and, to their credit, it is said that they nearly equal the genuine article and sell it much cheaper. If the contents of your pocket should be so limited as to require a second-hand suit, Church street is the place to be accommodated with one which has just left the back of either an honest workingman (who, through adver-

sity, has been forced to part with it) or the contracted
shoulders of some crack-brained dude, who sold it in
order to buy another that would still more imitate the
butterfly. The same applies to everything else. It is a
blending of everything in the shape of habitations upon
its long and crooked length, and the most eccentric boa-
constrictor never twisted itself into more crooks and
turns than this remarkable thoroughfare, commencing at
Water street and running far into the country. There
exists a kaleidoscopic array of churches, synagogues,
hospitals, grave-yards; dry goods, boot and shoe, furniture (new and second-hand) and grocery stores; meat
markets, stables, liquor houses, bars, undertaking establishments, human hair stores, junk stores, alligator-tooth
jewelry establishments; and so much out of proportion
to the size of the city as to surprise the best-traveled
stranger. In architectural effects, as far as variety is
concerned, the street by no means has to take a back
position; for not only are the five great orders invoked
and used without any regard to order, but a great many
new types and styles have found their way into this
happy architectural confusion. Some of them, I am
satisfied, could not be classified even by a committee
composed of Michael Angelo, Inigo Jones, Sir Chris-
topher Wren and H. H. Richardson. The first building after leaving Water street that I found of sufficient
interest to describe is known as

ODD FELLOWS' HALL,

an attractive-looking structure in the mediæval English
style, which rejoices in a grand display of great win-

dows and pinnacles, and contains the lodge-rooms of the Norfolk members of the three-great-links fraternity, as also a well-appointed theatre, styled the Opera House.
My next halt was in front of

OLD ST. PAUL'S CHURCH

and church-yard, which combine to make the most picturesque spot in Norfolk, and in point of historical interest, as well as real attraction to the tourist, its great heart, mind and eye-centre. Its inscribed tombstones, stained by the many changes of weather that a century and a half has witnessed, and the old time-tinted walls of the church building, imbedded with memorial tablets, plainly show that they were placed there when Virginia was a struggling colony, and speaks well for the early settlers, who made the best and most enduring building the one in which they worshipped God, for it stands to-day the only authentic artificial creation in Norfolk that by nearly fifty years antedates the Revolutionary war. The church was built in 1737, the material is brick (burnt in England), and which, as I have before stated, time has colored and toned to such perfection that it commands pure religious respect in place of simple admiration. Dense masses of ivy cling to its weather-beaten walls with loving, inseparable tenacity, its north side being so thoroughly mantled with this evergreen creeper that it makes a particularly impressive picture; while its south wall gives a chapter of Revolutionary history in the form of an imbedded cannon-ball which, it is alleged, was fired into it from the deck of the Liverpool, a frigate that, in common with the rest of the British fleet, was bombarding the city. Everything about the quaint old church-yard displays taste; the fountain, whether dry or throwing crystal jets to the breeze, looks as if it stands just where nature intended it to be placed; the old tombstones, the grass, flowers, shrubbery and trees, so perfectly blended, causes one to wonder how a space so flat could be made so picturesque.

Nearly opposite the upper end of this church-yard stands the

CENTRAL PRESBYTERIAN CHURCH,

which is a large, massive-looking edifice, constructed of pressed brick, trimmed with brown stone, and still further decorated with a well-designed porch of the same material. It has a well-proportioned, handsomely-slated spire that can be seen for many miles, and enjoys the proud distinction of looking as well upon near inspection as at a distance.

A little above this I came to a

HEBREW SYNAGOGUE.

The building is of the Grecian type, and has a Corinthian porch, something unusual in a Hebrew place of worship, for they have supplied the United States with the best specimens of the Moorish and other Oriental styles, which naturally add much, on account of their being unlike any other, to the architectural attractions of a city. I found that the reason they made an exception to the rule here was because the building had been erected by the Methodists for their own use, and then, for some reason, they sold it to Norfolk's "chosen people."

The next point of interest was the hospital of

ST. VINCENT DE PAUL,

one of Norfolk's greatest blessings—in fact, her

GOOD SAMARITAN.

Its heroic front of pressed brick, with immaculate marble trimmings, its mansard story, the well-selected shrubbery, noble trees and the graceful promenades that surround it, are all dedicated to the unfortunates who have lost God's greatest blessing—health. In its generous-sized wards many a fevered brow has been soothed and many a dying man has been reconciled to meet his Maker. I have heard that great Pickett, who braved the shot and shell of so many of the battles in which the Army of Northern Virginia was engaged, and led, on the bloodiest day at Gettysburg, quietly and peacefully departed this life within its noble interior. The building, outside of its history, is well worth seeing, being of excellent design and well built; the grounds are not only ample, but also tastily arranged and well cared for. The hospital, although under the supervision of the Sisters of Charity (and as a consequence is a Roman Catholic institution), limits its good work to no particular denomination, for its sweeping arms of charity and hospitality are wide open to the sufferers of every creed and every clime.

From here on the street makes many more curves before it reaches

THRIFTY AND TIDY HUNTERSVILLE,

for which it not only acts as Church but also Main street. The greatest feature of this remarkable avenue, as well as of Huntersville, and which is destined to become one of Norfolk's great attractions, is

LESNER'S GARDEN,

which promises to be one of the most extensive east of Cincinnati, and more remarkable, probably, than any in even the Western cities, from the fact that it combines the leading features of nearly all of them. It is, on a small scale, a zoological garden and also a flower garden. Art is represented by a number of iron and terra-cotta casts, some of them quite heroic, and a number of large halls give ample room for assemblies. The peculiar and permanent nature of the street-front of this attractive pleasure park first attracted my attention and its really quaint appearance further centered my gaze. It is in the form of a building of such large proportions that it overshadows everything in Huntersville. The first story is a pleasing combination of granite, marble, sandstone and pressed brick. The next is of wood, pierced with large windows, which have every appearance of being put there to admit light into a public hall; and above that a niche, filled by a statue, gives it quite an ecclesiastical appearance. But the most remarkable of all is the tower or outlook. There was certainly considerable originality used in its design, for I must certainly admit that in all my wanderings I have never seen any approach to it, elevation being gained by a number of cottage-like structures, one fitting the roof of the other, the height being one hundred and ten feet.

I walked in and found myself in a large hall, the centre being occupied by a permanent fountain, which, with its many sprays and jets of water splashing and trickling into its ample basin, will do a great deal, in connection with the three arches at the extreme end (which have every appearance of breezy tunnels), towards giving it the much-desired cool and refreshing aspect during hot and dusty July and August. Through these three arches I got the first views of the beauties of the garden proper, and without delay I walked into it. Upon reaching it I found first a unique terra-cotta vase, next a well-kept lawn. In the centre, upon a rustic base, stands a giant elk, with all the dignity and pose of a presiding official. This fine specimen of the deer suggested to me the name of Elk Lawn, and the magnolias which bordered it Magnolia Circle; a path which forms the interior boundary, and is ornamented by a line of evergreens, Evergreen Walk; and the companion walk on the other side, Zoo Ramble, as it passes the cages filled with wild animals. These names were adopted by the proprietor, who accompanied me in my walk over the three broad acres. As I looked at what has already been done, and observed the walks, well-arranged trees, well-kept lawn, pretty flower-plats, fountains, ponds and shady bowers, and then walked upstairs into the main or entrance building and found a well-arranged spacious hall, particularly adapted for musical entertainments, I could not help but think that Eastern Virginia and North Carolina, as well as Norfolk, had been "supplied with a want"; and when I considered its possibilities, I was satisfied that nothing stands in its way of becoming, not only a leading resort, but one of national reputation. I have seen many smaller ones North and West whose names are household words. As I was leaving, the proprietor asked me to give one item to the public. I do it cheerfully, and that is, that it is intended as a resort for ladies and children as well as gentlemen, and that no intoxicating liquids will, under any circumstances, be sold or allowed on the premises.

From here Church street still goes on, but only as an average regulation country road.

CHAPTER V.

DESCRIBES THE WATER-FRONT AND THE TERMINAL POINTS OF A NUMBER OF GREAT RAILROAD AND STEAM-SHIP LINES—AND CONCLUDES WITH WATER STREET AND ITS MANY INDUSTRIES.

Norfolk is rich in views which combine land, water and moving craft, and, although she has no noted docks like many European cities, or projecting stone piers or other triumphs of marine engineering, still there is much to interest one on the shipping front of this old port. I commenced the description of

NORFOLK'S WATER-FRONT

from the foot of Botetourt street, because here the first bridge crosses Paradise creek, and the two small streams which form it, and which are destined to become more conspicuous in the near future, can be seen from this point as far as they are navigable. The view here, although not striking in either scenic or shipping effects, is very diversified and pleasing, and has every natural advantage for great improvement. Up stream, or rather streams, many fine residences and the many trees in the whitewashed walls of the distant cemetery; on the opposite shore, the quiet pastoral scenery surrounding several large estates; down stream, innumerable sloops and schooners, and the saw-mills, packing-houses and lumber-piles of Atlantic City, complete the picture. A walk of one block to York street and another to its foot brought me once more to water. The scene here is far more active and beautiful; the bridge across to

ATLANTIC CITY,

and at its end that thriving little suburb, with its variety of industries and many small stores; inland, York street, with its many stately dwellings; to the left, the park-like grounds of the West End mansions, which have a water-front, and their solid stone retaining walls, as well as a glimpse of the harbor and the church spires of Portsmouth.

From here I sauntered to the water terminus of Butte and Free Mason streets, and then down to Granby, past the brick walls alluded to in another chapter, to a group of iron-plated buildings, one of which, by a large sign, indicates that it belongs to the

NEW YORK, PHILADELPHIA AND NORFOLK R. R.,

and by another, that it contains some of the offices of that road within its iron-clad interior. This, as well as a number of roadways and masts of distant shipping, convinced me that I had reached its tidewater terminus, as also the Norfolk end of the

NEWPORT NEWS AND MISSISSIPPI VALLEY R. R.

In order to look at these great interests intelligently, I concluded to take the first plank walk I came to. I was happy in my choice, for to my right I found the beautiful grounds of time-honored estates, luxuriant in trees and grasses; while to my left and front the scene convinced me that I had now reached the wharves devoted to the heavier carrying trade of this port, the basin, which ends at the foot of City Hall avenue, with a number of schooners discharging oysters, wood and coal, and between it and the walk a number of roads and car-tracks, the latter increasing to such a wonderful confusion as I advanced that it was surprising how the powerful locomotives, continually pulling the heavy freight cars, could possibly find those they needed. Thousands upon thousands of staves, which looked as if they might have exhausted forests, were neatly piled everywhere, awaiting shipment to Brazil and other South American nations. The plank walk abruptly ended at a warehouse which is now under process of reconstruction.

As I observed a large number of small masts and heard a continual noise at my right, I walked that way and found, to my surprise, a number of

OYSTER-PACKING HOUSES,

that I never knew existed, and the little cove, formed by these small wharves and the large one I was on, literally jammed with sloops and schooners discharging the delicious bivalves. Stuck away here, where few, unless they have direct business with them, ever see them (or, for that matter, ever hear of them), are a number of establishments belonging to one of Norfolk's leading industries, employing hundreds of hands.

I kept up the wharf, and from the extreme end enjoyed a good view of Atlantic City, as well as the palatial residences of that part of the West End bordering on the water. I walked around the warehouse of the Newport News and Mississippi road, which occupies the end of this pier, and then followed down the slip used jointly by it and the New York, Philadelphia and Norfolk road for their heavy railroad barges, and then went over to the substantial warehouse and wharf of the last-named company. Here I found a roomy landing and the space between it and the adjoining wharf (Boston) literally packed with huge foreign sail-ships and ocean steam transports from different climes, filling their holds with the great Southern staple—cotton.

In my exit from this centre of miscellaneous freight I passed the same iron-coated buildings and then resumed my stroll down Granby street to Main, and down that thoroughfare to

BOSTON WHARF,

which is very generally conceded to be the busiest in the city, for not only do the steamers of the Merchants' and Miners' Transportation line discharge and receive their cargoes of manufactured goods and raw material here, but two of the busiest compresses, during the cotton season, with the army of men required to run them, as well as the thousands of huge, clumsy bales that enter their yawning mouths to be reduced to a more convenient size and shape; and monster sailing-ships and steamers, the majority booked to sail for Liverpool and London, storing the snowy-looking cargo into their pit-like holds;—all combine to make this a scene of business activity seldom equalled and never surpassed on the American continent. More cotton is handled, as well as shipped to domestic and foreign ports from this wharf than any other in the city.

As I had seen the shed and landing of the Baltimore Steam Packet Company, I left here and went direct to

WATER STREET,

which follows most of the harbor-line, and shows sufficient variety in both buildings and the wares stored in them not to be in the least tiring. It is not only the leading street for the sale of goods of a nautical nature and the storage of material consigned to foreign countries, but also the leading wholesale and manufacturing street of the city. These varied industries are not mixed, but appear to be confined to districts. In order not to neglect any part of this most important artery, I walked to the water's edge, and was treated with a magnificent view of the

HARBOR AND SHIPPING.

To the right, first a fringe of masts and smoke-stacks, then projecting Lambert's Point; a little distance farther I could plainly see the magnificent water-way that leads to the roads, the bay and the ocean, the narrow but deep space between Lambert's Point and the opposite shore partially filled by a large ocean steamer which, as if abhorring the vacuum, concluded to fill the upper space with smoke and the lower with foaming water. I could also see reliable Cranie Island. Directly in front, the grand Ionic porch of the Marine Hospital and the surrounding park looked particularly striking; a little to the left I observed Portsmouth, with her many church spires; farther on, the Navy Yard, with a few specimens of our combative marine; and last, Berkley, as if thrown in to complete the scene, which, after enjoying for a while, I turned my back upon, in order to inspect Water street, which finds a beginning between the well-constructed iron warehouse of the

SEABOARD RAILROAD

and the property of the Shippers' Compress Company. For some distance from here the buildings are not very prepossessing; in fact, with just two exceptions, the houses of this important part of the city look very indifferent until the lawn at the back of the post-office is reached, when there is a change for the better, for here commences the backbone of the city's trade,

THE WHOLESALE BUSINESS.

Well-known firms I found everywhere, and at

COMMERCE STREET,

which is also filled with solid brick structures of leading wholesale and commission houses, it can fairly be said that the very heart of the city's heaviest business is reached. At

ROANOKE AVENUE AND SQUARE,

which is another hive of wholesale business establishments and equally solid commission houses, I was attracted by a slip which was packed with the favorite conveyances of tide-water truckers, schooners and sloops. They formed such a busy and unusual picture that I could not resist the temptation of becoming a closer observer; so walked to them.

After retracing my steps to Water street, I continued down that miscellaneous avenue, and after crossing Market Square I found a complete change. The wholesale feature appeared to have dropped out of the street and been replaced by small stores, which in turn give way to manufacturing establishments on one side and on the other the large storage warehouses, wharves and sheds of the great steam-ship lines that receive and discharge passengers and freight at this port. When I reached Taylor street

TWO LARGE WAREHOUSES

claimed my attention on account of their solid appearance and size; they are of the modern pattern, with large arched doorways, and look the very embodiment of solidity. One is occupied by the Merchants' and Farmers' Pea-nut Company, and the other, which covers an entire city square, and is the largest brick building in tide-water Virginia, is occupied by the Norfolk Storage Warehouse, the largest pea-nut concern in the world. On the opposite side of the street I observed a number of establishments which, in a marine town, are veritable

MARINE MUSEUMS,

junk stores. In passing one of these I found in front of it, used as a sign, the safe of the unfortunate Huron; it was utilized as a pedestal, for upon it stood the figurehead of a British bark that went down in the treacherous waters which lash the coast near Cape Henry. After inspecting these store-houses of faded glories for a few moments, I walked once more to the water-side, and found myself in front of the six hundred feet of Water street owned by the

OLD DOMINION STEAM-SHIP COMPANY.

Here was a continuous line of drays pouring out of the wide-open gateways, loaded with every imaginable kind of manufactured goods, and an equally large number driving in with cotton just picked from fertile Southern fields and pea-nuts from the adjacent counties, as well as all kinds of passenger vehicles, from the conventional hack to the fashionable barouche, filled with expectant friends—some ready to greet returned relatives, who had been far away on pleasure tours; others, to welcome to our hospitable shores industrious immigrants. I knew that this was one of the greatest of the coast lines, and realized that Norfolk was probably its greatest distributing centre, and that here are landings for its steam-boats that displace the waters of North Carolina's sounds and rivers as well as those of Virginia; but with all this knowledge I had a very poor conception of the amount of wharf-space and ground occupied by these extensive carriers and their perfect facilities for handling, storing, loading and unloading the great quantity of freight consigned to them. When I walked into the gateway I found myself in a well-paved plaza; I crossed it and looked at the two great piers and their capacious slips, and soon concluded that there was no better place to study the shipping interests of this port than on the magnificent property of this transportation line. I first looked at the many boats tied to the wharf-fronts. The "Accomack" was discharging pea-nuts and cotton raised in the valley of the Nansemond river, and behind her the dainty but fast "Luray" was hospitably receiving passengers and storing freight for Hampton and Newport News; while the "Northampton" appeared the very picture of impatience as she headed for her landing in order to contribute her cargo, gathered on the eastern shore of Virginia and Maryland. At another wharf I found the reliable "Pamlico," which has made so many successful pilgrimages through the Albemarle and Chesapeake Canal and the great sound after which she is named.

I next stepped into the

MONSTER WAREHOUSES,

filled with a literal wilderness of freight, drawn as if by a magnet to this centre from every corner of the globe. Huge blocks of mottled stone from the rugged mountains of Tennessee, statuary marble from sunny Italy, oranges from the groves of Florida, rice from the marshes of South Carolina, iron ore from New River (Virginia), portable and stationary engines from the machine-shops of New York, pianos from Boston, plate-glass from Paris, lime from London, tons of coffee from Brazil, and nearly as much tea from China; within a few feet of the last a lot of wild canvas-back ducks, who had made their last flight over Currituck Sound; and fish from near the mouth of the Chowan and Roanoke rivers. I did not intend to enumerate, for to describe the great variety of articles that I observed in these warehouses would require pages. My object for giving these few and those following is to show how well these giant freight receptacles and the wharves and shipping will repay a visit; what food they furnish for a studious mind; how they show what a prominent part the leading transportation lines hold in our economy by furnishing cheap, quick and safe transit to both raw material and manufactured fabrics; for here I continually found manufactured articles consigned to a certain place hundreds of miles away, and near them some of the raw material of which they were made, from the same locality, awaiting shipment to the same manufacturers, notably the following: Hides from Virginia marked to the Bay State, and shoes from Lynn for various parts of the Old Dominion; cotton from every Southern commonwealth tagged to the metropolis of New England, and huge boxes of calicoes, muslins and lawns from the looms of Massachusetts consigned to every one of the same States; marble from Tennessee for Boston, and soda-water fountains made at the Hub legibly directed to a number of mountain towns of western Tennessee.

The depth of water at the wharves is, fortunately, sufficient to allow any of the company's ships to come and go with full cargoes, from the smallest, the "Breakwater," of one thousand tons burden, to the superb and powerful last addition, the "Sennaca," which registers three thousand tons.

Opposite the front of the Old Dominion property are massed a number of foundries, machine-shops, ship smithies, and other metal works. I continued on past a marine railway and a ship-joiner's yard, and then found myself in front of

THE CLYDE LINE.

This well-known and far-reaching Philadelphia steam navigation company has here three piers, six slips and three wharf-fronts to accommodate its extensive business, and seven of its best boats, I believe, are required to carry the freight of its patrons in and about Norfolk.

From here Water street is bordered by a number of well-known iron works on the land side and sheds and warehouses on the water to its end at the well-improved estate of the

NORFOLK AND WESTERN RAILROAD,

which, judging from what I saw, I should say is the largest property-owner in Norfolk; neither has any other corporation or individual contributed as much to landscape features and the improvement and beautifying of the city. Their well-constructed wharves and large brick warehouses, with a range of neat gas-lamps, have an air of solid business. The huge grain elevator, with its many pockets and complicated machinery, filling the hold of a Spanish steamer, is of as great interest upon close observation as its outlines are at a distance.

The granite and iron bridge across the South-east Branch is the finest structure of the kind in or near Norfolk. The elevated roads, with heavily-loaded cars dumping coal into many bins, the silvery-looking network of bright steel rails, the substantial round-house, the handsome passenger depot and park, all combine, with the great foreign ships, steam-boats and coal-tugs, to make this a fit terminus for the shipping street of Virginia's great seaport.

CHAPTER VI.

WHICH TREATS OF GRANBY STREET—THE ALBEMARLE—VIRGINIA CLUB—CHEERLESS WALLS—GRANBY STREET METHODIST CHURCH—NORFOLK'S GREAT AND ONLY ART GALLERY—THE CITY HALL—CITY HALL AVENUE AND BANK STREET.

As Granby street can fairly be called Norfolk's street of great expectations (for a large number of her citizens believe that it will ultimately become the leading retail and fashionable shopping street of the city), I concluded to make it, in conjunction with a few others, the subject of a chapter.

This street, like many others in this city, on account of a grievous oversight or lack of judgment of her founders, abruptly ends at Main street instead of seeking the water-front for its southern terminus. The first block, on both sides, after leaving Main street, ranks with Norfolk's very best business houses. The west side is almost entirely occupied by one of the fronts, which includes the main entrance, office, spacious reading-room, billiard hall, barber shop, etc., of the Atlantic Hotel; while the other side is composed of a number of substantial store-houses, which terminate with what can justly be called the finest business structure in the city. The building, I regret to state, is not large, and is known as

THE ALBEMARLE.

The upper floors are utilized as an apartment house, and the rooms *en suite* contain every convenience known to the modern constructor, decorator and plumber, while the lower floor is occupied by a crockery establishment. It is very generally conceded as being the handsomest store in tide-water Virginia; but its fronts are its chief attraction, for nowhere have I seen terra-cotta used to better advantage, or more harmoniously blended with pressed brick, iron and colored glass. It looks as if its designer intended to make the lower floor a business parlor and the upper into apartments to suit even the fastidious taste of a French tourist. Its elaborate exterior and well-appointed interior bear witness to the fact that he succeeded.

Opposite this handsome structure stands the substantial building occupied by the

VIRGINIA CLUB.

I have seen many costlier, more pretentious and statelier club-houses, but I have never seen one that could better adapt itself to the seasons, for its well-lighted, handsome parlors look warmer in winter than most others, and no apartments look cooler or more breezy in summer. The members of the club are gentlemen who have had the good sense to correct some of the errors into which other clubs have unwittingly fallen, as it is less exclusive to strangers whose literary or social merits are acknowledged than the celebrated Somersett of Boston or Westmoreland of Richmond; and an honest Virginia hospitality is dispensed which is exceedingly refreshing in an age when people are too prone to gauge the man by the amount of capital he commands.

After crossing a narrow street, on the same side, I found myself in front of

A STATELY MANSION,

evidently belonging to a building period which, as far as Norfolk is concerned, has passed into history. It is adorned by one of the best Ionic porches I have ever seen, the columns resting upon a solid paneled stone platform. Without doubt the well-kept green lawn and modest fountain in front of this building do much to give it its dignified appearance; yet I candidly believe that the general harmony displayed in the embellishment of cornice, railings and even chimneys make it an architectural example well worthy of study by our home-builders of the present period.

A few steps from this *ante-bellum* palace brought me to where, in rapid succession, places of interest are passed by the pedestrian. The first of these, I am sorry to say, is anything but a pleasing rest for the eye; it is made up of two of the

MOST SELFISH-LOOKING WALLS

that it has ever been my province to behold. They are opposite each other, and are built of brick and whitewashed. One of them, I judge, has a frontage on this, one of the most prominent of Norfolk's streets, of about three hundred feet, and the other fully, if not over, four hundred and fifty; and, unfortunately for the city's appearance, they enclose the finest grounds within its limits. These walls have often been the cause of very ludicrous blunders, and furnish no little food for the practical joker. It is said that an observing tourist, having been informed that Norfolk had two interesting cemeteries, and that they were enclosed in whitewashed brick walls, concluded to take a street-car ride, in order to get a good idea of the city and its leading streets, and then visit them; but when he got to these rather unnatural enclosures (for residences) he stopped the car, alighted, and walked towards the nearest gate, evidently thinking that he had reached the cemeteries, and that it would suit his convenience to take them in first. He found that he was mistaken when he looked through the gateway and beheld the magnificent, park-like grounds which surround the neat, well-cared-for and cheerful-looking residences.

I am satisfied that some of my readers will consider it wrong for me to write as I have of these walls, because they are private property; but I am confident that when they reflect, and realize that they are forced upon the public gaze, and that this book is intended as a faithful gazetteer, to point out disadvantages as well as advantages and the ridiculous as well as the sublime, they will say that I was compelled to notice them. Some, I fear, may even go further, and think that I was guided by hostile feelings towards the owners; if they do, they are certainly mistaken, for I can conscientiously state that I am not personally acquainted with either, not even knowing their names. I have no doubt they are most excellent citizens and have the city's best interests at heart, for the grounds plainly show that they are the fortunate possessors of both taste and refinement; but I candidly affirm that if they will remove these prison-like walls and replace them with a neat iron railing they will receive the grateful thanks of their fellow-citizens and add much towards beautifying their city.

This is the only part of my manuscript that I permitted any one to look at, for my rule in writing has always been to take no advice or suggestions from any one; but for fear that I might offend private individuals who had done me no harm, I read it to two gentlemen (one of them being one of Norfolk's best-known journalists) and asked them if they considered it in any way objectionable. They both agreed that there was no ground for offense, and further assured me that they also had been surprised that the owners permitted them to disfigure their magnificent grounds.

I had to walk only a few steps further on to find the street once again redeemed, for, commencing at the end of one and opposite the other of these gloomy walls, I found a number of

OLD–SCHOOL SOUTHERN MANSIONS,

which follow each other in rapid succession. They make a most refreshing contrast to the cold and cheerless places I had just passed. The side-walks are skirted with trees; the front yards, although not so spacious, are ample, and (best of all) can be seen and gladden the eye with their green carpets; the buildings are all of brick, and are large and roomy. They all difier materially, though they plainly show that they were constructed about the same time. Every one of them has an air of comfort. Wide stone steps lead up to hospitable-looking doorways. All, with one exception, have porticoes which show that the Virginian of old not only studied the classics, but also made his knowledge useful, for the first has Ionic columns, the second Doric, and the third Ionic; then follows the exception, the one not supplied with any portico. It appears to be older than the others, for it belongs to the Colonial period, when white marble panels, with sculptured garlands and protruding heads, cut out of the same material, were considered the grandest effects for exterior decorations. Opposite these, stands another of these survivors of a past age. A handsome porch with Corinthian columns is the leading feature about the building, and two quaint and curious-looking brick erections at each limit of the front grounds give it quite a feudal appearance.

On the next corner, after crossing the street named in honor of our first President, I had an opportunity of looking at the

NORFOLK COLLEGE FOR YOUNG LADIES.

The appearance of the Granby street front is solid, spacious and neat, but any one who has heard that it has accommodations for over three hundred pupils, and that light is admitted by one hundred and thirty-six large windows, and that it has twenty-seven class and recitation rooms, outside of those used as dormitories, is very prone to be disappointed by its appearance; but all doubt will be dispelled when he walks up Washington street and looks at the spacious annex. The front is composed of two lofty stories, built of brick, and a well-designed mansard, making in all three stories. The location is elegant for the purpose, being healthy and accessible; and best of all, it has a reputation for efficiency and for imparting a thorough education second to none in the country.

The large front yard (of No. 129), in which a magnificent magnolia, bits of rush, and broad, velvety lawns represent nature, while a large, life-like bronze mastiff and neat fountain of the same material represent art, next attracted my attention, and caused me to make a mental calculation as to how many citizens (compelled to stay in the city during the summer months) blessed the proprietor as they looked over the low, unobstructing iron railing and feasted their eyes upon the refreshing green.

A few steps brought me to the corner of Free Mason and

THE GRANBY STREET METHODIST CHURCH.

It has a fine front, consisting of four magnificent Ionic columns, which support a well-proportioned and well-designed entabliture. So far so good, if the architect would only have stopped there; but, unfortunately, he did not, for from the roof springs what was evidently intended for a church steeple, which looks very much as if the designer intended to cap the building with a cut between a Moorish tower and a bee-hive, but just before its completion changed his mind and concluded to gain elevation by adding a shingled pinnacle. With all candor I must admit that distance lends beauty to this colossal pile of framed lumber and swamp shingles, and it does not look quite as awkward and displeasing to the spectator who is far enough away not to distinguish the material employed in its construction. The interior, I am glad to say, makes up to some extent for its faulty steeple; the ceiling of the auditorium is elaborate and in good taste; stained glass of excellent design fill the windows, and the acoustics are perfect.

From here I continued on to Central Market, a neat iron-plated building, where the majority of the well-to-do inhabitants of the West End look for their supply of meat, fish and vegetables. From the side-walk in front of this, I stood for a few moments to admire

NORFOLK'S GREAT, EVER-CHANGING ART GALLERY,

which occupies a front, I should judge, of a little over one hundred and fifty feet on Butte street, about the same on Charlotte and about eighty on Granby. Nearly every circus in the United States and nearly every itinerant theatrical company, as well as lecturers on phrenology, psychology, botany, etc., patent medicine houses, sewing machine, piano and other manufactories, spend incredibly large sums of money to keep up this grand picture gallery. Here you can see, one day, a train dashing along at night, a man tied to the track, and a young woman, with hair as red and conspicuous as the rays of the locomotive's head-light, releasing him just as the engine-wheels are about to dissect him! Next week it is replaced by a steam-boat explosion, with a hero and heroine going up so high that it takes them a week to come down, and then not of their own accord, for they are pulled down, ruthlessly pulled down by the sticky hands of an unromantic bill-poster, so that their place might be taken by a critical-looking old gentleman, who fondly looks at a bottle of whisky of a certain brand, or the benevolent-looking phiz of a gentleman who is about to deliver a lecture on the evils of intemperance.

My reason for thus describing the bill-boards which face three of Norfolk's best streets is to call the attention of the good citizens to the fact that this is the nearest approach to a public art gallery that the city has, and with the hope that they will profit by it, and that a number of its most cultured and wealthy citizens will form themselves into a society for the purpose of securing this or some other conspicuous site for the erection of a much-needed gallery for the display of the finer arts, so that Norfolk's rising generation will have something else to draw artistic inspiration from besides the daubs representing cut-throats, Indians and jig-dancers. I respectfully submit this, as it would do incalculable good.

As these boards are at the end of the street, I retraced my steps to

CITY HALL AVENUE,

which enjoys the distinction of being the widest in the city, and citizens point to it with pride as a street that, through the agency of enterprise and hard work, has been reclaimed from one of the tidal streams which are such a prominent feature in the geography of this well-watered city; and it is said that at the extreme inland point of this avenue a man was drowned only a few years back. After more buildings are placed upon its front it promises to be quite a picturesque street, for at one end, in a well-constructed basin, considerable of the small craft, particularly oyster schooners and sloops, which are owned or seek trade at this port, relieve the monotony by their graceful models and tapering masts; while at the other, towering above all surroundings, stands the

CITY HALL,

which is the second finest building in the city. Its magnificent row of gigantic Doric columns, springing to a great height from a base reached by a number of broad stone steps, and supporting a well-proportioned pediment, looks exceedingly well, and from the centre of the roof eighteen Doric columns support a majestic dome, which does more to give Norfolk the appearance of a city, from any point of view, than any other building within its limits. It makes no great display of outside ornaments, but what it lacks in them it makes up in the solidity and quiet dignity of its appearance.

Two courts meet in this plain but artistic edifice, which is surrounded by

THE ONLY PUBLIC PARK

or square that the city, as yet, has improved. It is a pretty lawn ornamented with a large-sized fountain.

From here I extended my walk to

BANK STREET.

The lower part contains a number of well-stocked retail stores, while the upper is lined with substantial dwellings, the majority of which, I am satisfied, will, before long, have to come down to make way for business structures.

There is one building on this street (No. 5), now in process of construction, which promises to be one of the most remarkable business edifices south of the Potomac; and when it is taken into consideration that it has a front of only eighteen feet and a depth of twenty-two feet, and that it is destined to become a wholesale and retail house and to contain the offices and the room for a manufacturing establishment, I know the reader will agree with me in calling it a veritable curiosity. As soon as it gained sufficient height to tower far above its neighbors, a great deal of concern was manifested by the passers-by, and many were the ideas expressed relative to its use. Some evidently thought that it owed its erection to a religious society who wanted to give an illustration of the Tower of Babel; others, that some antiquarian had concluded to present to Norfolk an exact copy of the Alexandrian Pharos; not a few thought that the government was putting up a combined light-house and signal station; while a shot-tower was the conjecture of some. One day, as I was conversing with the proprietor, he sent for the architect's drawing of the front elevation. The scale plainly indicated that it would overshadow all its surroundings; and, taking into consideration the adverse circumstances which surrounded the designer, it is a remarkably effective front. The owner wanted room; the architect realized that the only way to get it was by digging down towards the empire presided over by the Tycoon or by climbing up to the clouds. He preferred the latter. The next question, evidently, to present itself was how to keep his eighteen feet front, twenty-two feet depth and over ninety feet elevation from assuming the shape of a Glasgow chimney or an enclosed pile-driver. That he succeeded is certainly very gratifying, for the front is bold, original and even dignified. It is a happy blending of different styles adapted under most trying circumstances. There is evidence that light, as well as display, was worked for, for from the ground-floor up to the two Moorish windows, directly under the well-designed pediment, it promises to be a massing of neat and highly ornamental iron columns and French plate and cathedral stained glass.

CHAPTER VII.

IN WHICH I WALK THROUGH FREE MASON STREET—LOOK AT AND INTO CHRIST CHURCH—THE BAPTIST—MASONIC HALL—THEN SAUNTER THROUGH NORFOLK'S FASHIONABLE DISTRICT, THE WEST END.

FREE MASON STREET

has always been considered Norfolk's centre of fashion and ideal place of residence; and although powerful rivals have been developed to share her social supremacy, particularly West Butte, York and other streets, which, with their palatial residences, assist to make up the fashionable West End, and Holt and East Main streets and Brambleton in the east, all of which contain the homes of some of Norfolk's most fashionable and illustrious residents, still, after careful research, I must say that, although the homes of the noted and wealthy inhabitants of Norfolk are pretty thoroughly scattered, many on streets not mentioned in this chapter, that if any street deserves the definite article as to being the most fashionable and containing the handsomest residences and other structures not erected for business purposes, that street is Free Mason. This fashionable causeway finds a very modest beginning at a very busy part of Church street; and on the first block, although the buildings are good and comfortable, I found none of sufficiently striking appearance or public interest to require description; but not so with the following, for on the first corner (north-west) stands

CHRIST CHURCH.

There is no building in Norfolk in which the exterior and interior are in stronger contrast than in this, and no structure more fully proves the old saying that "there is but one step from the sublime to the ridiculous," but in this case the sense is reversed: the outside is ridiculous—the inside is sublime. There are only two things about the exterior of this edifice that are well designed—the large, well-shaped cathedral windows and the elaborate iron fence which encloses the grounds. As for the building, it belongs, strictly speaking, to the age of plaster, its stuccoed surface being laid off in squares, evidently for the purpose of making the near-sighted believe it is stone. From the pediment springs what looks like a huge dry-goods box sawed to fit the pitch of the roof; then another dry-goods box, with a lonesome-looking clock in it, which has but one dial, and that exposed only to Free Mason street, as if time was useless to the rest of the community; then a circular tower, and above that a shingled pinnacle. The man who stands in front of this building and concludes to walk inside will be well repaid, and if he is not astonished at the magnificent interior, after viewing the outside, it will be remarkable. Everything about it has a pure and sacred tone; the light is dim and (in a religious sense) perfect, and is admitted by large windows filled with magnificently-executed cathedral stained glass; the ceiling is handsomely frescoed, and the reredos, its crowning glory, is a most effective study.

A walk of one block more brought me to the

FREE MASON STREET BAPTIST CHURCH,

which, in my opinion, is the most thorough and best ecclesiastical architectural study in the city or (as far as I have seen) in the State. It is, however, as ridiculous in material as it is grand in design. It has that dignity and thorough religious look which accompanies the early English Gothic, and its massive, square-pinnacled tower and side elevations, so well conforming with buttresses and pinnacles, would easily be taken for some English parish church, created in the seventeenth century, if it were not for the fact that slight differences in the color of the stucco and a few cracks in the same coating show that the building is not stone, but brick plastered to imitate that material. If it was built of stone, which the design naturally calls for, it would stand without an equal in either of the Virginias or Carolinas. As it is, it will well repay a visit.

At the next street crossing I found that one corner was occupied by the

MASONIC TEMPLE,

an edifice by far more conspicuous on account of cost, size and elevation than architectural merit. It is unquestionably a solid building, and without a doubt well constructed; its pressed-brick front looks very smooth and very red; but I venture to say that if a stranger were informed that Norfolk was the fortunate possessor of a fine watch or cigar factory, and was sent out on a voyage of discovery to find it, the very moment his eyes would rest upon this huge pile of brick he would exclaim, "I have found it!" for it certainly looks a great deal more like some of the new model factories, where little or very light machinery is used, than an ideal temple. Yes, there was honest and neat work done when the building was constructed, but its appearance is decidedly too commercial for a temple in which are held the secrets of centuries and mysteries unfathomable.

On the corner of Granby street I observed a large mansion with a high outlook, which, in connection with the Granby street church, makes this part of the street look quite prominent. After leaving here I passed

LEACH–WOOD ACADEMY,

a most excellent institution. The building is of brick and terra-cotta, partially covered with ivy, and looks well.

At Bush street Free Mason enters and forms a part of the

ARISTOCRATIC WEST END,

where it, as well as the rest of this centre of wealth and fashion, presents a grand array of domestic architecture. Fine buildings and well-cared-for grounds follow each other in such rapid succession that attention is called only to the most striking and best specimens. Even this, I fear, will be considered

DRY READING,

but I deem it necessary, under the circumstances, to enumerate in order to do justice to Norfolk and to show the studious stranger, in quest of information, that this part of the city is well worth visiting. Any one not fond of reading the purely descriptive, I can assure, although I've not had the advice of counsel on the subject, that there is nothing in the statute books of the State of Virginia to show that their skipping over to the next chapter would be considered a breach of the peace or any other kind of misdemeanor. The system I have adopted is to give the numbers, where I could see them, and where I could not, to describe their location as plainly as possible.

The building material employed is, unfortunately, very generally limited to brick with terra-cotta trimmings in the better class and wood in the poorer class, a stone front being a rare exception. On account of the many styles employed, and the lovely grounds which surround many of these dwellings, I found that this district, fortunately, lacks that which ruins many more pretentious residence sections in much larger cities—monotony.

Free Mason street does not go into this favored section with much architectural flourish, but gradually gets more pretentious—in fact, changes from extremely-cramped old age to a later period, and finally to the present day. One of the boundary corners furnishes a site for an old wooden colonial-roofed building which looks as if it might have been the headquarters of any number of Revolutionary heroes, and the opposite corner has a row of substantial-looking bricks, which makes a fair attempt, through the agency of a mantle of plaster, to look like stone.

Nos. 97 and 99 are handsome buildings, their fronts neatly relieved by terra-cotta, bay windows, dormers, and mansard roofs. No. 61 is of brick, of the old English pattern, ivy-clad, with high stoop and Doric porch, and would be a magnificent companion to those on the corner of Bank street.

On the north-west corner of Duke and Free Mason stands a large Italian-looking structure with an abundance of balconies and lofty outlooks. The yard is nicely laid out and is a receptacle for rare plants. No. 72 is a pleasing structure, bordering on the Queen Anne style, and a pretty yard shows that the proprietor's taste runs towards nature as well as art. No. 70, now in process of construction, promises to be, when completed, the handsomest residence in the city; it is to be entirely of Seneca sandstone, relieved by polished granite. Lots 48 and 50 are occupied by a stately mansion three stories in height, with a magnificent Ionic porch; a pretty fountain and urn, occupying each a grass plat, add much to its appearance.

The block of buildings, three stories high, from 26 to 36 inclusive, are particularly noticeable, as they are unlike any other on the street.

On the north-west corner of Botetourt, I found

THE MOST PICTURESQUE RESIDENCE

in the city. The entrance is an arch covered with ivy and the great bay window in front is overgrown with the same evergreen, neatly trimmed so as not to interfere with the light. Its picturesque broken French roof, pierced with many well-designed dormers; its magnificent grounds, which run to the water's edge, filled with flowers and trees in which the cedar and magnolia blend their branches, must be seen to be appreciated. Free Mason street most appropriately ends here at a stone retaining wall, lashed by the waters of the harbor.

From here I strolled to

WEST BUTTE STREET.

This beautiful avenue, like Free Mason, commences at the water's edge. The first building is a handsome new structure, while on the opposite side is a very solid-looking one of the old school, surrounded with ample grounds, shaded with different kinds of large trees and further adorned with urns, lions, and the huge bones of a whale which make an archway for a boat-landing.

The south-west corner of Botetourt is particularly noticeable. The building is adorned with a pretty porch with Corinthian columns, but its main attraction is the grounds, which contain handsome gold-gilt urns with growing plants, a fountain of unique design, and surrounded by a neat iron railing with gilded tips. This lot, though small, ranks among the most attractive in the city. The grounds which surround No. 35 are also relieved by a fountain and handsome urns. No. 37 is a new pressed brick with spotless marble trimmings.

On the corner of Dunmore street I observed a block of buildings in process of construction which promises to rank among the best.

On the square bounded by Butte, York, Dunmore and Duke streets stands just one house. It has a commanding appearance, being tall and stately, has a well-filled conservatory, and is probably the largest residence in the city.

Nos. 81, 83, 84 and 88 are good specimens of comfortable modern homes, and do much towards giving the street its fine appearance. No. 108 is a cosy new structure, and the grounds on the south-west corner of Duke are very attractive. The building sufficiently resembles the one described on Botetourt to cause any one to believe that they were both modeled in the same "form." The tips of the neat enclosure are also gilt, and there are lovely urns, while a large, handsome fountain, but of different design, throws its cooling sprays into a basin surrounded by small urns.

Diagonally across from here I noticed a substantial block of four pressed-brick marble-trimmed buildings, the white marble steps which lead to the different entrances faced with the same material and stained glass.

On the north-west corner of Bush street is a building (now receiving its finishing touches) which is admired by all who pass it. In its construction a good plan has been well executed, and stone, terra-cotta and black cement have been harmoniously blended.

One block up Bush and I found myself on

YORK STREET.

No. 150, on this street, is a neat brick building, with windows which contain much stained glass, and has a mansard roof composed of tiles and slate. The building which stands on lot 116 is not remarkable itself, but so much taste is displayed on grounds which are arranged so as to allow many pretty glimpses that I could not help mentioning it. Art and assisted nature have certainly done well here.

The large block between Yarmouth and Dunmore streets is occupied by eight well-designed separate buildings, each differing, and standing a short distance back from the street-line. The intervening spaces permit of small grass plots, which are well taken advantage of.

No. 18, the last residence on the north, is an elegant new mansion. Its mansard, pierced by many windows, was well planned, and evidently, in part, to insure the best water and city views that unfold themselves here.

The south side of the street ends with a pretty little private park, well laid out. The proprietor evidently belongs to the unselfish class who believe in beautifying the city in such a way that the public can enjoy the green grass, flowers and trees on his estate as well as himself, for a very low fence is the only thing that intervenes between the pedestrian on the city's side-walk and this property.

The water vista from this point, although not by any means the best in the city, being somewhat blocked by Atlantic City on one side and part of the West End on the other, permits a good view of a very interesting part of the harbor, which carries upon its glistening waters everything that can float, from a fleet, dainty yacht to a slow, lumbering scow; and from a steam war-ship that, with thundering volleys, announces its arrival, to the screaming tugs, which dash about in every direction. These, with the tall spires of the Portsmouth Memorial and Catholic churches, which can be seen at a distance, and Atlantic City, which is just across the bridge at the very foot of the street, as well as the noble estates, with their magnificent broad, shaded and grass-carpeted grounds, held back by solid stone walls from the grasping waters, make a fit ending to Norfolk's prettiest and wealthiest district—the West End.

CHAPTER VIII.

WHICH IS RATHER SOLEMN—FOR IT DESCRIBES CUMBERLAND STREET, WHICH LEADS TO NORFOLK'S CITIES OF THE DEAD—AND CONCLUDES WITH A DESCRIPTION OF THESE INTERESTING BUT MELANCHOLY ACRES.

No street in the city gives the same food for solemn reflection to the citizens of Norfolk as

CUMBERLAND STREET,

for be he professional man, mechanic or laborer, he knows that his last ride will be through this street; for when the first lays aside his legal-cap, the second his tools, and the last bids eternal leave to his labors, be he rich or poor, white or black, the last roadway, intended for the living, that his remains will pass over before they are deposited within the white-washed walls of Norfolk's Campo Sanco is known as Cumberland street.

The street, unfortunately for the city, the city's trade and the convenience of citizens, does not have the waterfront for a starting-point; but although it commences at a street which looks narrow and forbidding, I did not have to take many steps before I found myself interested in and viewing the

CUMBERLAND STREET METHODIST CHURCH,

which here displays its substantial front. It is of the Doric order, and possesses two heavy flights of granite steps, which reach a solid platform of the same material that supports two solid columns and with them makes an impressive entrance to a well-decorated interior.

A few feet further up on the same side brought me to the

CUMBERLAND STREET BAPTIST CHURCH.

It is a clean, neat-looking building, and belongs to the same order of architecture as the one just described, and, although of the same general design, differs materially, from the fact that it has no granite platform. Its two Doric columns support a pediment within which a well-designed panel informs the public, in letters of gold, that it was erected in 1816, while two pretty grass-plats in front of the structure add much to its general appearance.

The reason these buildings interested me so much was because everything about them bear the impress of solidity, and they are fine specimens of the Grecian style and Doric order without ridiculous embellishments, now rapidly disappearing.

A short distance further up brought me to

CUMBERLAND CASTLE,

a rusty, two-story-and-basement stuccoed construction, evidently created for three purposes: First, to show how ghostly a look a habitation intended for the living can possibly have; second, how best to display sixteen columns where they can do the least good; and third, how ridiculous the Doric order used in the Italian style can be treated.

As I was gazing at its abandoned-looking front, a gentleman walking by informed me that it was named Cumberland Castle, and that this street, one of the most interesting in Norfolk, was actually named in honor of this wreck; but I am satisfied that this is a mistake, and that the street was called after the brother of Charles the Second, the Duke of Cumberland, who commanded the victorious army at the battle of Culloden. The street up to here I found possessed good and comfortable habitations, built of brick and wood, and occupied by white citizens; it continues the same way up to East Butte, after crossing which it becomes the

COLORED FREE MASON STREET,

as it is given up to the recognized *bon ton* of the colored population as a place of residence.

On the corner of Suffolk I came to a substantial, well-designed brick structure (occupying, with grounds, an entire square), which gives evidence that it was intended and well adapted for school purposes, and upon enquiring found that it had been erected by the city of Norfolk for her

COLORED JUVENILES.

This certainly does not look as if the South was opposed to the education of the negro.

A few steps further, and I stood in front of

CEDAR GROVE CEMETERY,

one of the three great burial-grounds of the city of Norfolk. The entrance, which fronts the end of Cumberland street, and is in fact the

MAIN ENTRANCE

to the entire system, is not, I am sorry to say, what it should be. It consists of four square piers built of brick, the only attempt at ornamentation being an arched recess in each and caps which look decidedly military, and which fail to give it that solemn appearance almost necessary in a cemetery entrance; in fact, the four cannon-balls on the tops of these business-like looking piers, and the general appearance of the entire structure, would force almost any one to believe that it is the gateway to a navy yard or the grounds attached to an arsenal or barracks. But the moment I stepped inside, the well-cared-for glistening shelled walks, the close-clipped grass, the waving cedars, and last, the mournful marble monuments, convinced me that I was on sacred ground.

This is the oldest of the cemeteries, and the monuments, although not particularly grand, are nearly all well designed and of imperishable material. The vaults are of the old pattern, some faced with brick, and all lacking the delicate traceries which the chisel has wrought upon the fronts of some of the late erections of that class of repositories for the dead in the great rural cemeteries scattered throughout the land; but none of these show the decayed and fallen-in appearance which is, unfortunately, so prevalent in old burying-grounds, and the many little grass-covered mounds show that care and attention is still bestowed upon them. In fact, I could see no evidence of neglect anywhere.

I walked up the main drive and walk (which, in an air-line, traverses the entire length of the grounds), and at the end found a gate, and upon walking through it cast my eyes upon a scene which few strangers, knowing the flat surface that Norfolk stands on, and having just passed through Cedar Grove (which, having no elevations save those made by the graves, looks particularly flat), is hardly prepared to find. This remarkable change in the landscape, which has natural features sufficent to insure fine park-like effects with very little outlay, is a decline or grassy slope to a tidal marsh abounding in rush and reeds, which even chill winter does not entirely rob of its wild beauty, and a corresponding upward slope towards the new cemetery. The marsh is crossed by a solid embankment which, having a graceful curve, is in beautiful contrast to the straight walks of the cemeteries. The stream is crossed by a substantial stone arch.

After looking at this scene for a few moments I walked over to

ELMWOOD CEMETERY,

and the very moment I passed through the regulation gate-way I observed (as far as the general plan and surface are concerned) that it is a duplicate of Cedar Grove: the same flat grounds, the same straight, stiff-looking walks crossing at right angles. It is, however, larger, has a greater number of trees (elm and cedar predominating), and the monuments are costlier, and, as a consequence, larger and more elaborate.

I realize that the majority of even the most enthusiastic citizens of Norfolk, when it comes to a discussion of how to make Cedar Grove and Elmwood equal in beauty to the great park-like rural cemeteries of the prominent cities both North and South, with their hills, valleys, ravines, grottoes, streams and lakelets, immediately give way in despair. But they need not do so, for although both are unfortunate in being laid out on the checker-board plan, instead of having serpentine walks and winding drives which permit of oval, oblong and circular lots, in place of the regulation squares which the first makes necessary, and which it is too late now to rectify, both cemeteries being too old (for when Cedar Grove was first dedicated I could not find out, it being so far back that no one knew the exact date, and as for Elmwood, it was opened in 1853, when the air was charged with that malignant scourge, yellow fever, and the great number of deaths caused hasty burials with little regard to landscape effects), I still say that, with all these difficulties to contend against, the two great cemeteries of Norfolk could be made most beautiful in a scenic point of view, and that, too, with little expense, by being thrown into one. The sought-for redeeming features are the slopes, salt meadow and tidal stream between the two.

The following advice, if acted upon, I am satisfied will give Norfolk a cemetery of which she would have a right to be proud: Take down the north wall of Cedar Grove and the south wall of Elmwood. This would not only give brick enough to substantially run down each way to the bank of the creek, and thus practically put both under one enclosure, but also have some to spare to help to permanently enclose West Point, the adjoining colored cemetery. The two white cemeteries thus made one would add, by their severe regularity, to the beauty of the scene; and the many light tints and shades of the monuments occupying the most elevated ground would make a splendid contrast to the deep green of the trees and other shrubbery that surrounds them. The intervening land, being uneven, gives fine scope for landscape effects and horticultural displays, and the water-way, by building a retaining wall (the outer surface moss, reed or grass-grown, in order to take away its artificial effect), could be utilized for a pretty lake.

Although these cemeteries look flat, they are anything

but devoid of history, romance or startling reminiscence. The memorials in Elmwood embrace everything in the form of sculpture, from the Gothic canopy, the Egyptian obelisk, or

"THE STORIED URN,"

made famous by Gray, to the equally touching and impressive tribute of the less wealthy—the simple inscribed slab; for the citizens of Norfolk have innate that noblest trait in the American character—the loving care for the dead. Cost is no consideration when the grave of a loved one is to be marked by enduring stone, and Elmwood shows it.

The first monument to attract my attention in Elmwood was that erected by the Masonic fraternity to

DR. UPSHUR,

who fell a victim to the yellow fever in 1855, while ministering to the sick who were afflicted with that disease. It is of marble, ornamented with scrolls, Father Time, the Virgin, broken pillars and other Masonic symbols, and is crowned with an urn encircled with a wreath of roses.

After leaving the grave of this heroic physician, I concluded to walk up the avenue which lies in front of it, and which is carpeted with soft green grass and shaded by a variety of trees, to the monument erected in memory of Mrs. Dickson, which is a magnificent floral design well executed in marble. From here, I found, on my way, many monuments which are costly and appropriate. At the end of this walk I turned to the right and proceeded down the main avenue to the enclosure of the

UNITED FIRE COMPANY.

In the centre of this is an appropriate marble monument, and the shields, bearing the letters C. S. A., over many of the graves, show that they faced other fire besides that of burning buildings.

Next in line, a path intervening, are the grounds of the

HOWARD ASSOCIATION,

that noble organization of ministering angels who are always first in the field when pestilence is abroad and death lurks in the atmosphere.

From here I sauntered down to the

WESTON MONUMENT,

which is unquestionably the handsomest in Norfolk. It is a highly-decorated Gothic structure. Three well-executed statuettes, acting as finials to three buttresses, well represent Faith, Hope and Charity; while under a most elaborate canopy stands a classically-robed statue, having every expression of sorrow, leaning on an urn which stands on an inscribed pedestal.

When I reached the gate I took the next path that led north, and soon found myself in front of the well-designed monument over the mortal remains of Miss Martha Berkley, which consists of a base with a life-size marble statue of a maiden leaning upon a cross.

I next found the

VEITH MONUMENT,

erected by grief-stricken children over the remains of an affectionate mother. Four polished granite columns are introduced in this structure, which is of marble, two of them capped by urns, the other assisting in the support of a canopy on which is cut a female arising from her sleep and an angel, with crown in hand, pointing upward. It is a grand piece of work, while the tangle of ivy, just above, looks as if the chisel might have been guided by a hand equal for execution to that of Michael Angelo.

After leaving this walk I found the most noticeable monuments much scattered. The Dalrymple, a fine paneled obelisk, and opposite, the one erected to Geo. J. Thomas, a soldier of the Confederacy, in a panel of which stands the figure of Hope on a cliff lashed by marble waves; the tall and well-cut memorial to Wm. H. Turner;—all on the same path and near each other, are well worth seeing.

On the very next avenue I found a beautiful granite obelisk to Dr. Tunstall, and another to that eminent scholar, Hugh Blair Grisly, LL. D.

On another path stands the polished granite memorial erected over the tomb of Mr. Kader Biggs, who was born in Williamston, N. C., followed by a handsome marble monument to the memory of young Gary Weston, on which, in a panel, is a draped female figure looking at a cross with an expression wonderfully sincere.

Many other monuments, both granite and marble, which the want of space crowds out of this little book, are worthy of mention, notably that of the much beloved physician, Dr. Thomas Nash; the beautiful polished granite stone in memory of Edwin Nash; and another to the wife of Mr. Thos. R. Balentine, a lady born in Currituck county, N. C.

One well-cared-for mound, particularly, attracted my attention, for it contains all that is mortal of one whose memory is not only held dear by the citizens of the State he loved and served so well, but also the entire South—the late

JAMES BARRON HOPE.

No memorial as yet marks the spot where this unselfish citizen, "unflinching journalist, patriot, poet and soldier" is interred, and I hope no monument will be raised by just the family alone, as I think the public have a right to become contributors. I am satisfied there is not a journalist or printer in Virginia or the Carolinas but would consider it a proud privilege to contribute towards building to him a monument of marble as pure and spotless as his character, and outside of the sanctum, the composing and press-room his friends are legion.

There are three plots occupied by societies that are very interesting. One is known as the

PICKETT-BUCHANAN CAMP.

The interments here are very few, and I sincerely hope that it may be so a long time, and that the "last taps" and the farewell volleys will not find an echo among the trees of Elmwood for many years. Many Confederate and some Federal soldiers are buried in family lots. Among them are a number of Confederate commodores and commanders, while near them two United States commodores are also resting peacefully. One of these died the year the war commenced, while the other, who departed this life in 1887, often, on Federal decks, answered with angry guns to a Confederate cannonade.

The second of these plots that gives food for reflection is that owned by the

SEAMEN'S BETHEL ASSOCIATION.

Here lie buried, far from their native homes, mariners who have died at or near Norfolk. The sixteen men who made their last voyage in the German ship Elizabeth, which foundered almost in sight of one of Norfolk's most noted pleasure resorts, also rest here in peace.

The other plot is

THE ELKS' REST,

the name being cut in legible and enduring letters upon a block of stone. In the centre of this well-turfed lot, which is marked by marble posts, stands a giant elk. I had finished my walk through the cemetery, and was on my way out when I observed this representation of the monarch of the North American forest, and concluded to get nearer. Acting on that resolution, I soon found myself standing under the shadow of his great antlers. It required no tongue to syllable the fact that

I was at one of the burial-places of that fraternity which, though organized only a few years back by a few actors, has now developed into an organization which extends from ocean to ocean and gives daily demonstration of the good that can be done by following the motto cut on the monument, "Brotherly Love, Fidelity, Charity and Justice." I am not a member of this brotherhood, but I cannot help but have admiration for a body of men whose first thought, evidently, is for the dead. The elk, elevated upon his lofty and substantial pedestal, looks the very embodiment of active life, and, thus surrounded by the dead, makes a remarkable and rather strange contrast. When I looked at this noble specimen of the deer tribe, with head proudly erect, appearing to breathe words of defiance as he surveys the surroundings, I could not help but think that the artist intended these words should be:

"Oh death, where is thy sting?
Oh grave, where is thy victory?"

CHAPTER IX.

WHICH IS RATHER SHORT—BUT COVERS CONSIDERABLE TERRITORY—FOR IN IT I WALK THROUGH HOLT STREET AND BRAMBLETON.

HOLT STREET

is divided into three distinct and wholly unlike parts. The first, from Church street to Chapel, is not remarkable for the grandeur of the buildings which line its fronts; the second, Chapel to Walke street, has a decidedly foreign look, caused in part by a number of theological structures, schools and charitable institutions massed together, instead of being in different districts, as is usual in this country. The most prominent of all these is

ST. MARY'S CHURCH,

which is the largest and probably the costliest in the State. Its magnitude can only be appreciated by viewing it from various points, the best being from the sidewalks of Holt street (a few feet east of the building), where it gives the fairest impression of its size, and also from Chapel street south of its front. The edifice is of brick, stuccoed, and the style is the decorated Gothic. Its steeple is very conspicuous, being the highest elevation yet reached by any structure in Norfolk, and its general effect would be very pleasing were it not that its greatest length is zinc or iron which appears to be appealingly looking for a coat of paint in order to conform in color with the rest of the building. The interior, however, makes up for many faults, for it commands the admiration of all who visit it, and the general verdict, irrespective of creed, of all who scan its three altars (the central beautified with Roman mosaics), its columns, capitals, busts of the evangelists, its magnificent roof and the great columns that assist in supporting it, its marble tiled floor, its organ loft, with the heroic and appropriately-decorated instrument, the stations of the cross, presented by members, each an individual study of merit in oil, consistently framed, and the many large stained-glass windows, is that it is a remarkably handsome interior.

A little to the rear, and facing Holt street, stands the old church, now used, I believe, as a school. It is a fair specimen of the Doric order and Grecian type.

On the corner of Reily street, in a large yard, well adorned with shrubbery, stands a mansion which has the most foreign appearance of any creation on the street. It is in the Italian style, and I am satisfied the architect must have got his inspiration from Norfolk's Cumberland Castle. Standing back in the garden which surrounds it, it makes a more creditable appearance than the parent structure. It was formerly the residence of the pastor of St. Mary's, whose individual property, I believe, it still remains.

Next to this I observed the building known as

ST. JOHN'S ACADEMY,

which has an excellent situation, but a rather awkward-looking tower. A Protestant orphan asylum comes next. It stands on the corner of Walke street. There are two more of these institutions which give a home and protection to the fatherless in this city—one Protestant, and the other, which also does good work, under the supervision of the Catholic Church.

From Walke street to the bridge, Holt has a

DECIDEDLY AMERICAN

appearance. On the north side I passed a number of pretty cottages. One near the water is very elaborate, and built of brick, terra-cotta and marble, with quite a display of colored glass. Each of these cottages has a small green in front, and the rustic fences which enclose some give them a very pleasing appearance.

On the south-east corner I noticed a palatial residence, one of the finest in the city. It is of pressed brick, plentifully faced with marble.

At the foot of this street I crossed the wooden bridge to

BRAMBLETON,

the latest addition to the city, now called East Norfolk. It is well situated between two lovely sheets of water— the one I crossed, which is known as Mahone Lake (and is, at high tide, well entitled to the term), and the Eastern Branch. It is already a pretty place, and when the trees which line nearly all its streets have the advantage of a few more years growth it will be remarkably handsome. Four of its many well laid out thoroughfares are already particularly noticeable. They are Willoughby, Park and Brambleton avenues and Lovett street. It was upon the first named that I found myself when I stepped off the bridge, and the first place that attracted my attention was the

HEMINWAY SCHOOL

and its magnificent stretch of green grass and original growth of stately pines, enclosed in a neat but substantial iron fence, which does so much towards beautifying this new part of the city.

The leading industry of this district, I should judge, after a ramble through it and observing the many acres of hot-houses filled with choice growing flowers, to be horticulture. Three florists have their gardens here.

Many wooden churches and two built of brick are already created. One of the latter is a pretty little Presbyterian church with a curious little belfry, and the other a Baptist with quite a handsome interior.

CHAPTER X.

WHICH IS VERY IMPORTANT, FROM THE FACT THAT IT DESCRIBES SOME OF NORFOLK'S MOST INTERESTING AND PECULIAR PLACES AND LANDMARKS.

In this chapter I wish to point out spots and places in Norfolk that are unlike those of any other city, and which are likely to indelibly impress themselves upon the stranger as being among the leading features of the city. The first and most prominent among them is

MARKET SQUARE.

It is not a city's public square in the usual acceptation of the term, but two streets, three blocks long, on each side of the principal market, and is, without doubt, during certain hours each day, the busiest and most crowded place, of the same area, in Virginia or the Carolinas, for not only does most of the population of Norfolk and suburbs do their marketing and shopping here, but at one end the two ferries which connect the two principal suburbs (Portsmouth and Berkley) pour forth masses of human freight to intermingle with this already dense crowd, and at the other end the street-car lines make a common centre, and it is also the only carriage, express and job wagon stand in the city. The well-stocked market is open every day from early morning to noon and on Saturday until ten at night. To see the huckster-stands and market wagons filled with the choicest of vegetables from the great truck farms of Virginia and North Carolina; the fish-stands, with the scaly products of the contiguous sounds, bays and rivers; game from the marshes of Currituck Sound, Chesapeake Bay and the great Dismal;—is a sight worth seeing on a Saturday night, when hundreds of smoking, glaring torches illuminate these same stands; all the rest of the available space being occupied by

STREET ORATORS

in carriages, each supplied with great blazing lamps and surrounded by crowds, which adds no little to the busy and remarkable appearance of the square. Some harangue the multitude by proving that they have soap that will even remove the stains from the character of a New York "boodle alderman"; or medicine that will cure every disease from corns to consumption; or microscopes with which a man can look through a foot of plank; or cement that will mend anything from the main shaft of an ocean steamer to a broken heart.

There is no place in Norfolk where a better idea can

be formed, by contrast, of her improvement since the war than by

THE TWO FERRY-HOUSES

which stand side by side at the foot of Market Square. Both are owned by the same corporation. One was built before the war, and is contracted, low in pitch, built of wood, and has a decidedly cheap appearance; is devoid of all ornamentation as well as comfort, and for years has been permitted to disfigure this site, which it does yet, but people are no longer forced to go through its unhospitable, barn-like quarters. The new one just erected and now in daily use has a lofty archway, and its outside, constructed of ornamental iron, has a cheerful look. Being of generous width, it is roomy and comfortable, has well-appointed waiting-rooms, and the interior is finished in woods from the adjoining Southern forests.

There are two street crossings in Norfolk which no stranger should fail to see, and though they are both made famous on account of the buildings that occupy the respective corners, they are so unlike that comparison would be ludicrous. The first combines all the stateliness, the solemnity and quiet of the most select, tradition-haunted quarter of an English cathedral town, while the other, with one corner excepted, has all the stir and blending of business that forms the prominent feature of the wildest and newest Western city. The first of these crossings presents, without question,

THE MOST PICTURESQUE COMBINATION

of buildings in Norfolk. It has a decidedly English look—in fact, has more the appearance of the genteel section of an old English college town than the majority of the cities of modern Britain can themselves produce. There is only one thing which would look strange there, but not out of harmony, and that is the well-developed magnolias which here spread their magnificent branches.

On the south-east corner stands a grand old residence, which looks as if it might have been occupied by some of the nobility before the Revolution, if it did not bear in very legible gilt letters the date of its erection (1798). A neat yard, embellished with a fountain and flowers, adds much to its appearance, and its front is ornamented with a pretty Corinthian porch. In the rear (a few feet back in the same enclosure) is a two-story brick of peculiar design, which should not escape the eye of the visitor.

On the opposite corner stands another old mansion, also of brick (of the glazed ante-colonial pattern). It differs materially in design from its neighbor, and looks considerably older. It also has a neat porch with fluted columns with Ionic capitals. In its capacious back-yard a magnificent magnolia casts its shade. No one should fail to walk up Free Mason street towards Brewer and look at the back of this quaint old building. Its peculiar-looking windows and its ivy-covered walks have a home-like appearance hard to imitate.

The other corner of note is that occupied by the Free Mason Street Baptist Church, which, with its dignified front and well-proportioned, pinnacled tower, finishes a picture that for quiet beauty, refinement, venerable appearance and solid comfort, without ostentation, is seldom seen.

The other crossing, as I have before stated, is as different from this as the mind can picture. I did not make the discovery myself, and probably would have passed it unnoticed if a friend had not pointed out to me the peculiar combination that forms the strange make-up of the crossing of

CHURCH AND COVE STREETS.

The latter should be called Curve street, for if there is any street that equals Church in crooks, curves and unnatural turns it is certainly Cove. The four corners formed by these two streets are very different in appearance and the use made of them; and, if it had been carefully studied, no establishments could have been devised to better work hand in hand. On one corner is a grocery store, well stocked with edibles to sustain life; on that diagonally across is a thoroughly equipped drug store, so that, if a man should arrive at that particular stage in his career where, through sickness, he should be prevented from eating, and that medicine must take the place of food, there is his medicine; and, if that should fail, directly opposite an undertaker has his shop and mysterious paraphernalia ready; while diagonally across is the solemn grave-yard which surrounds old St. Paul's Church. Thus, on these four corners, every leading step in life is represented—active health, sickness, preparation for the tomb, and the tomb itself.

Norfolk, to a considerable extent, is a city of surprises, but I never was more surprised than when I walked up James street and found that this street, which is almost entirely occupied by people who, though honest and industrious, certainly do not belong to the wealthy class, and small retail stores, possesses the only

"MAGNOLIA-SHADED SIDE-WALK"

in the city. These magnolias are planted at the outer edge of the side-walk for over three hundred feet. They were put there by an eccentric French florist who owned the grounds back of them, on which he has a literal forest of magnolias. It is known among the neighbors as

THE MARTINS' REST,

for the reason that in summer hundreds of thousands of these birds make them their resting-place at night. It is a sight to see these great armies of feathered wanderers darken the sky as they circle 'round this little forest and then to shoot down as if they were so many arrows; so rapid is their descent that many every night get killed by the concussion in their eager haste to find a resting-place.

Personal observation has shown me that there is no city in the United States where the

COLORED POPULATION

have better opportunities for advancement or gaining a livelihood than in Norfolk; and there is no place on earth, not excepting Africa's Liberia or America's Massachusetts, where they are safer in the possession of their property, can make an easier living, are better clothed, or attend to their own business more than they do in Norfolk; and, last and best of all, are better housed. Although they live in different parts of the city, the majority are massed in that remarkable network of streets which lie north of Charlotte, east of James, west of Church, and south of the cemeteries. A good many of the new houses are neat two-story brick buildings (with two-story kitchens attached) and are intended for two families. The main thoroughfare occupied by them is

QUEEN STREET,

and is unquestionably one of the best situated in the city, and, with the increase of the city's population and wealth, it is destined to become one of its leading business avenues. At the present time it is not only the promenade, but also the main business causeway of the colored population. Although it has no great buildings, there is much to be seen and to study on this street. The best time is between six and ten on a summer evening. It is then the colored people, being released from labor, don at once their happy dispositions and good clothes, and the dusky belle strolls coquettishly with the fantastically-dressed, dark-hued dude, or they scatter the dust, in one of the many improvised dance-halls, with their delicate "plantations."

There are a large number of

COLORED CHURCHES

in the city. The most conspicuous stands on the corner of Bank and Charlotte streets. The exterior of the structure is quite pleasing, the leading attraction being a large rose window. It is said that it will be the fortunate possessor of a very high steeple; up to the time of this writing it is only a little above the roof-line, patiently waiting for the congregation to raise more money to give it the intended elevation.

CHAPTER XI.

WHICH IS ADDRESSED TO THE CITIZENS OF NORFOLK AND THE ADJOINING CITIES AND VILLAGES IN GENERAL AND SUBMITTED TO THE BUSINESS PEOPLE OF THE SAME IN PARTICULAR—WITH THE HOPE THAT IT WILL BE HONORED WITH A CAREFUL PERUSAL, AS IT TREATS UPON BUSINESS, PARKS, EXISTING DISADVANTAGES—AND, MOST IMPORTANT OF ALL, GIVES A FORMULA FOR THEIR REMEDY.

In writing this book it was my intention to limit my descriptions to the architectural, physical and other attractive features of the city of Norfolk that would be of interest to the stranger, ignoring trade statistics, and mentioning great buildings and wharves in place of the business transacted in and on them, thus making it a guide to existing things in the form of a narrative, in order to relieve it as much as possible of the direct and technical descriptions which prove so tedious in books of this class. But when I walked through its streets, and became better acquainted with its hospitable people and studied its natural advantages, I became thoroughly interested, and the more interested the more

PUZZLED:

Puzzled as to how a city, standing upon a site selected over two hundred years ago (1681), laid out in the same year and inhabited ever since, and the wisdom of the choice never having been disputed, has not a larger population. Puzzled, that being situated in latitude 36° 50' 50" N., the most favored part of the Temperate Zone, with the great Gulf Stream nearer to her than any other city of note in the world, thereby further tempering her climate; with an ever-open waterway to the ocean; with a harbor so thoroughly locked against destructive wind and wave as to be as safe as a mill-pond in the fiercest storm;—that she has not a greater transatlantic trade. Puzzled, that with the advantage of natural inland navigable water-courses which are without a parallel in the world; with Chesapeake Bay making both shores of Maryland and Virginia directly tributary; with the Delaware and Chesapeake Canal bringing the Delaware water-shed within its grasp; having, through the agency of the Rarritan Canal, sheltered inland navigation to the Hudson river, Erie Canal and the great lakes; with the Potomac, the James, the Rappahannock, the York and other streams further assisting to bring to its doors the products of Virginia, Maryland and the immediate West and North; and from the South, through that triumph of engineering, the Albemarle and Chesapeake Canal, throwing into her lap cotton, naval stores, lumber, etc., from the sound and many of the river counties of North Carolina;— that she is not a greater inland distributing centre and does not enjoy a greater wholesale trade.

I know that this is not a popular way of writing, and will be considered by some quite out of the usual routine, as the greater number of articles which treat on Norfolk show very plainly that the authors believed that the only road to success lay in an endeavor to flatter its population into the belief that the city has made wonderful strides in population, trade and wealth, in spite of the fact that the site of Norfolk and that of

THE SECOND LARGEST CITY

on North or South American soil was selected the same year, and there is no person, endowed with average judgment, who will look at the map, but will admit that the situation of Norfolk is superior to that of Philadelphia; yet the census of 1880 showed that the population of Pennsylvania's metropolis that year was 846,984, while that of Virginia's favored port was only 21,966. In 1840 the city of Chicago contained 4,479 inhabitants, but since that date she has raised herself twelve feet above the mud of an Illinois prairie, reversed the course of a river (so as to throw her sewage into the Mississippi to keep from polluting her water supply), lost two hundred million dollars by one fire, and came forth more vigorous than ever for a struggle for first place among the cities of the nation.

I write this, the reverse of the usual style, without any hesitancy, because I am satisfied that every sensible man in Norfolk will agree with me in saying that her people should realize her capabilities and advantages, and all should unite in making Norfolk one of the greatest cities on the globe. I will readily admit that I never would have touched on this subject if I had only diagnosed the disease, but having discovered a remedy, and owing Norfolk a debt of gratitude, I concluded to give her the benefit of the formula.

No matter which way I walked I could see some feature that, if properly taken advantage of, would add to the greatness of the city. Then the question would again arise: Why a port with a situation for commerce equal to New York or Liverpool; for the manufacture of cotton goods superior to Manchester or Lowell (on account of the raw material growing up to her very corporate limits); why, with lines of silvery rails to the coal and iron fields of the mountains of Virginia and West Virginia, and with a large number of other railroads and water transportation lines zealously working in her behalf, she has not made greater strides on the road to comparative prosperity with the great trade and manufacturing centres of the continent. It did not take me very long to find the cause, for it soon becomes apparent to the most superficial observer. It is this:

NORFOLK IS LITERALLY WALLED IN

by her suburbs, which appear to have raised a barricade to prevent her growth, and up to this date, with one solitary exception (Brambleton), have been unquestionably the greatest disadvantage she has had to contend against. The inhabitants of these surburban cities and villages must certainly know that individually their corporations never can become great cities, and, as a result, cannot realize good values or sufficiently profitable usage for their estates; yet many of their inhabitants oppose every attempt to make this one municipality, when even the most illiterate stranger possessing reasoning powers can see at a glance that the only way for Norfolk and her suburbs to get the full measure of their greatness is by

ANNEXATION,

thereby throwing all into one civic system. The way the matter now stands, Norfolk and her surrounding cities and towns are the central figures of unquestionably the best representation (on American soil) of the

CELEBRATED IRISH CAT FIGHT

which made Kilkenny famous. On one side of the line we find Norfolk, on the other the suburbs, and as they scratch and fight the great cities of the Atlantic seaboard laugh, and as they laugh they grow fat at their expense; but it's rough on the cats.

"What will we gain by annexation?" is the question continually asked by the inhabitants of the suburbs when that subject is discussed. The best way to answer is by pointing out what has been lost thus far by the cut-throat policy which has been pursued for more than a hundred years; and I think a few examples, drawn, to some extent, from actual occurrences, will serve best to show that the claim that new transportation lines looking for a terminus, inventors looking for sites to erect factories, and wholesale dealers looking for places to locate are guided by population is not problematical, but an undeniable fact.

First: One of a company of California's greatest capitalists is in search of a tide-water terminus for a great system of railways. He is attracted by the advantages afforded by the deep and well-sheltered waters at or near Norfolk. Before locating the necessary wharves, freight-houses, elevators, etc., he is asked whether it would not be advisable to cross the James and thus have the advantages afforded by the city of Norfolk. He replies that to a railroad running from ocean to ocean a city of only 21,000 people (as represented in the census of 1880) is not taken into consideration when it comes to locating a terminus, as the business created by the road should soon make a city nearly as large, and they would have the profits accruing from advanced land values. He is then reminded that Norfolk and her immediate suburbs have over 60,000 population.

"That is even so, but you must remember that it is a house divided against itself," is the reply, accompanied by a knowing wink.

Second: A successful Northern wholesale merchant, who is forced, for his health, to seek a more genial climate, concludes that Norfolk, as far as situation is concerned, is the right place. He looks at the census of 1880 and despairs, but research shows him the population of the suburbs. He pays a personal visit and finds all the ill-feeling existing between them which is the natural offspring of a number of corporations situated side by side with interests nearly alike. As a consequence, he goes further South and locates in Charleston, South Carolina.

Third: A large company, being impressed with the advantage that Norfolk has in tapping the gold leaf tobacco belt of North Carolina through the agency of the Seaboard Air Line, takes into consideration the location of a great tobacco factory in Norfolk, but is induced to locate in Richmond because it has a larger population.

These incidents (with probably the first an exception) continue to repeat themselves, and I give them to show that annexation is not simply a question of sentiment, but profit; for the greater the parent city grows the greater, naturally, must be the prosperity of her annexed suburban children.

Another advantage this union would afford would be a system of parks and drives which would not alone be a pleasure and health-giver to the resident population, but would also, by attracting visitors, aid the growth of this united city. Her equable climate would make her a great winter resort. All that is necessary is for her to make herself more attractive, and, with her two railroads reaching the sea-side at Virginia Beach and Ocean View, it would be hard to find her equal as a summer resort. But as I speak of parks further on, I will now hastily review the suburban cities and towns that should form part of this grand municipality. The first and greatest is

THE CITY OF PORTSMOUTH,

which had, in 1880, 11,388 inhabitants. It is well laid out, its streets being wide and of good length, two of them (High and Court) being particularly noticeable. Near the junction of these two, but on Court, stands the Confederate monument, constructed of granite from the celebrated Linehan quarry of Vance county, N. C. Its extreme height is fifty-six feet, and when it receives the four bronze statues which are to represent the various branches of the Confederacy's combative service it will rank among the most artistic, dignified and imposing in the nation.

The city is flanked on the south by the Navy Yard, with its solid granite million-dollar dry-dock, its well-appointed, well-designed and well-constructed buildings, crowded with novel machinery and powerful engines, its interesting naval museum, its well-kept walks and pretty lawns; and on the north with the United States Marine Park, with its wealth of trees and shrubbery, and solid stone sea-walls, well-calculated barriers against the encroachments of the greedy waters of the harbor.

Portsmouth, in a historical point of view, does not by any means take a rear place in the rank of American cities. Laid out in 1752, and made a town the same year by an act of Virginia's Colonial Assembly, she peacefully accumulated population and wealth up to the Revolutionary war. Early in that eventful struggle for liberty Lord Dunmore retreated from the then capital (Williamsburg) and raised the royal standard within her town limits. She was captured after he abandoned her by General Leslie, and finally became the headquarters of that worst and most justly abused of all Americans, Benedict Arnold.

During our great fratricidal struggle Portsmouth (as also Norfolk) was at different times in the hands of both of the contending armies. The destruction of the Navy Yard and the Federal fleet anchored at its front, and the subsequent building of that marvelous home-made marine triumph, the ram Virginia, which the emergency of the occasion, home designers and mechanics brought to such wonderful perfection that she not only reversed the usual style of war-ships, but is to-day considered as having been a marvel, both in model and construction, by the best naval architects of all nations.

Berkley, Huntersville and Atlantic City, which also belong to the galaxy of corporations which should be made part of Norfolk, have been partially described in other parts of this work. The first and largest was formerly called Washington, and has enjoyed the distinction of being the county-seat of Norfolk county. It is well laid out and has a number of marine railways, but it owes most of its prosperity to the improvements made by the

NORFOLK SOUTHERN RAILROAD,

that great corporation which, backed by energy, push and far-seeing intelligence, has by degrees established its depots in nearly every city, town and village in Eastern North Carolina—reaching them by rail when possible and by steam-boats when necessary.

Huntersville promises to be more famous when the new pleasure garden, described elsewhere, is opened to the public.

Atlantic City has often been invited by Norfolk to become part of her, but has so far coyishly declined, the reason for refusal being that she was afraid that her powerful neighbor would not give her fair play, evidently thinking that annexation was a gorgeous parlor, Norfolk a monster spider, and she a delicate fly. Norfolk, on the other hand, believes that Atlantic City is entirely too modestly named; that only one ocean, and that not the largest, is not sufficient to give an estimate of her idea of her own grandeur and importance, and that she should be named The World, as it is supposed that this earth we inhabit is about all she wanted in return for becoming part of Norfolk; and some people think that if Norfolk had had the power to concede this modest request, and had done so, she would have insisted that two or three constellations from the planetary system should be thrown in for good measure.

The great trouble with Portsmouth appears to be that she is afraid of losing her identity and thereby the record of her early achievements. But I do not think that should cause her anxiety, as it can be easily remedied by throwing the annexed portions into districts and allowing them to retain their original names, as Boston has done. Another reason is because a wide, deep river separates the two; but other cities have crossed as wide, navigable streams and thereby increased their importance and influence. Boston crossed the Charles and swept into her limits historical Charlestown, which contains Bunker Hill, upon which took place the celebrated fight that will never fade from the pages of history; also the heroic granite shaft which commemorates the event, her other monuments, public squares, statues and fountains, and her great navy yard. She also annexed Dorchester, from whose heights Washington forced the British to evacuate; crossed the harbor to get in Noddle's Island, and crossed more water to increase her territory by depriving South Boston of the cardinal point in her name, in order to make her part of the city.

Philadelphia had no hesitancy in jumping across the Schuylkill or Cleveland the Cuyahoga. Baltimore is on both sides of the Patapsco. Chicago, with her nearly forty miles of wharf front on her rivers, is looking for more.

Brooklyn has made herself the third largest city in the United States by annexing the city of Williamsburg, and it is very generally conceded that the day is not far distant when New York City will quietly reach across East river, take her under her municipal wing, and, thus united, become the second largest city in the world.

Another and incalculable benefit that should be the outcome of this union is

A PARK SYSTEM,

intelligently planned upon a broad and liberal basis.

The citizens of Norfolk, as well as her suburbs, have been negligent as to public grounds, but they have the opportunity of forming a consistent system of parks and park-ways which would be the admiration of the world.

I write opportunity based upon this reasoning: The land can be acquired with little cost and most of it probably at no cost. They can make the improvements, which always require the greatest outlay, at a trivial expense, on account of the material required for them being near at hand, in inexhaustible quantities and at the lowest prices, and can be delivered at many needed points by water. The improvements are the drives, walks and paths; the material, oyster shells.

This can be accomplished by drawing a line commencing at the water-front just outside of Atlantic City and continued on just a little outside of the corporate limits of that place, also Norfolk, Huntersville, Berkley and Portsmouth.

Don't make this an imaginary line, but construct a grand avenue or boulevard, three hundred feet wide, leaving two hundred for park purposes and fifty on each side for street uses. Back of the parts most densely populated and most accessible to the majority of the people this could be reinforced by doubling the amount, thus giving it a width of six hundred feet. It should end just outside of the beautiful government marine park, from which a pier should project far out into the water, as well as another on the opposite side, in order to give citizens and strangers an opportunity not alone to behold the grand water views and the outgoing and incoming shipping, but also to add health and comfort in summer by health-giving breezes.

I know that numbers of people believe that the land in and about Norfolk is too flat to permit of any remarkable landscape gardening, but I am satisfied, after an inspection of parts of it, that there is no greater opportunity for making one of the grandest systems of parks and drives in the world at a nominal cost, which would grow in beauty every year, as improvements could be added annually, and the trees which it would be necessary to plant would develop in time to magnificent reaches of growing woodland, in which all the species that grow in Virginia and North Carolina would blend their leaves, and the many tints form that glow which warms the heart and makes man forget his trouble. Nor will any park in the world show more well-sheltered waters, adapted by nature for pleasure boating, or give better opportunities for thoroughly matured, elaborate landscape gardening; for this magnificent and nearly circumnavigating chain would cross many beautiful tidal streams with graceful shores, many of them already possessing beautiful, sloping banks and extensive meadows, with the rush and reed so peculiar to tidal waters, ravines, low hills, wooded slopes and groups of great trees, thus giving every opportunity for drives and bridle and foot-paths, past charming scenery, embracing water views, valleys, hills and dales possessing sylvan retreats, grottoes, green lawns, masses of shrubbery, and the many water courses covered by handsome bridges and bordered by pretty landings would give thousands an opportunity of reaching this creation, which would honestly deserve the quotation, "*Pro bono publico!*"

It would be still better to commence this avenue from a new pier just outside of Lambert's Point. This would give a length of about ten miles to these parks and park-ways.

Just one thing more is absolutely necessary to make Norfolk appear to the stranger, as well as the citizen, a beautiful city, and that is by changing the appearance of Market Square, for it is here that more people concentrate and more strangers form their impression of Norfolk than anywhere else.

The removal of the market and using the space it occupies for a public park has often been suggested and as many times bitterly opposed, the oppositions coming mainly, I understand, from gentlemen who own the stalls in the market; but I think that this could be equitably arranged by building a new and greater market and giving them the choice of the stalls. The strip thus released could be made a semi-tropical garden, for lovely magnolias could grow in it, delighting the eye with their matchless green leaves and loading the air with their fragrance, and other plants that could not thrive in higher latitudes, while in the centre

A MONUMENT,

towering above all surroundings and vieing in grandeur and artistic merit with the greatest testimonials ever carved out of marble or granite or moulded in bronze, should be erected to perpetuate the deeds of the heroes of three wars: The men of Norfolk who lost their lives while fighting Dunmore at Great Bridge during the war of the Revolution; the volunteers who prevented the capture of the city during the war of 1812 by their desperate and successful defence at Cranie Island, and last to the Norfolk soldiers of the Southern Confederacy, who for four long years fought in a cause which looked hopeless from the first and followed a flag which, though never recognized by the nations of the earth, has gained the respect of even its greatest enemies on account of the fortitude and self-sacrifice of its followers and the heroic deeds enacted on both land and sea under its folds, now forever furled.

Norfolk's opportunity for creating

A MARINE PARK,

or rather an embankment, is not altogether lost. It is easily made possible by buying the strip back of the estates in the West End, from the foot of York street to near the Newport News and Mississippi Valley Railroad wharf, and moving the retaining walls further out, thus securing a magnificent drive and promenade, bordered by the handsomest, best laid out and most artistically arranged grounds in the city on one side, while on the other the ever-moving waters of the harbor, fretted with black hulks, white sails and curling smoke, moving gracefully and seemingly keeping time to the music made by the waves gently lashing the sea wall.

NOTE.—The annexation of the suburbs is no new thing. It has been agitated, I understand, and fondly looked for for over thirty years, and I think there is no better time to accomplish it than now and no better way than by the system of parks and park-ways which I have suggested and submitted in this chapter.

I can further say to the citizens of Norfolk that this is not planned in the interest of any land scheme, as I do not own a foot of ground in any of the places mentioned and have never spoken to any one upon the subject in or out of the city.

CHAPTER XII.

CONCLUSION.

I have nearly finished my task. It was hastily constructed and many circumstances combined to make it a work of less magnitude than the subject justifies and which more cheerful circumstances would have made it.

While considerable sickness in my family, and the death of my little child, gave me an opportunity of seeing how ready the good citizens of Norfolk are to soothe and watch by the bedside of the sick (and I am grateful for this opportunity to return thanks for their honest hospitality and sincere friendship), still these adverse circumstances and trouble naturally had anything but an inspiring effect. A great deal of unavoidable work in and outside of the literary channel forced me out of the city when it would have been to the best interest of this book for me to have stayed; and assistance, as far as descriptions were concerned, was impossible, as I had promised advertisers and other patrons that every city and town would be written up by myself and backed by personal observation, and if I had not it would have been the same, as I have always held that the lowest of all swindlers is the thief who will knowingly allow another's brain-work to come out under his name. But

THE END IS DRAWING NEAR,

and I take a last, lingering look at the city I have described from an upper window of my High street home. The trees have been rendered leafless by the gentle touch of cold which accompanies winter even in this balmy climate, save the near little forest of magnolias which refresh the eye with their ever green and ever pleasing color; hence my view is unobstructed. I glance at the meadow between me and the small tidal stream called Paradise creek and then my eyes rest on the opposite shore, which consists of about two hundred yards of uncultivated land, the foreground relieved by a large-sized open boat picturesquely decaying and the remaining space covered with wild grasses and still wilder looking rush. The land slopes gently upward to the city, which is solidly massed in a long line in front of me, looking at this distance more than ever like some ancient English cathedral or college city, with the Baptist church, its square, solid and pinnacled tower, centrally situated and standing in bold relief, the dome of the City Hall and the many church spires that overtop the roofs of Norfolk.

As I pen these closing lines

DARKNESS

gradually mantles the earth, and spires, domes, turrets and houses recede from my sight like a dream, but I linger until Night, with her great dissolving power, has taken full possession and removed every outline of the distant city. I then make a light, and the first thing it brings legibly before me is the title-page of my book, which causes me to muse and think until I become satisfied that if, on some future day in the next century, when this great nation will have the Arctic Ocean as its only northern boundary and the Panama Canal will mark its southern limit, it should be the fortune of one of these books to survive and fall into the hands of an author whose province it is to describe the city, he will smile at its modest title, "Norfolk; the Marine Metropolis of Virginia," as he boldly names his work—"Norfolk; the Marine Metropolis of the Republic of United North America."

THE END.

DIRECTORY

OF THE MAJORITY OF

NORFOLK'S LEADING BUSINESS HOUSES.

The following names and addresses, under appropriate headings, are, a list of the majority of the leading business houses of the city of Norfolk.

I do not claim that it is complete, or that it is altogether the fault of the business men of Norfolk that it is not, as I did not have time to see all of them.

There is one thing, however, that I can say without a particle of hesitancy, and that is that no names appear except those of firms and individuals that are, as far as honest dealing is concerned, absolutely beyond reproach, my object being, from first to last, rather to lose twenty patrons than to get one that is questionable or unreliable; the result being a directory which I can place before consigners and purchasers with this assurance: that although all the good business houses of Norfolk have not been reached, *none have been reached but those that are good.*

(For the Press, Attorneys, Dentists and Photographers, see Press and Professional Lists of Norfolk, Portsmouth and Eastern North Carolina).

Agricultural Implements.

C. Billups, 101 and 103 Water street.

Agricultural (Shell) Lime.

Nottingham & Wrenn, 56 Main street. (See advertisement).

Billiards.

M. Hofheimer, 207 and 209 Main street.

Beef, Mutton, Pork, Sausage, &c.

S. S. Dann, Central Market, cor. Granby and Charlotte streets.
Wm. F. Dann & Co., 22 and 24 City Market.
L. Wasserman, 1 and 3 City Market.

Canal Companies.

Albemarle and Chesapeake, Franklin Weld, President. (See advertisement).
Dismal Swamp, John B. Whitehead, President.

Crockery and Glassware.

S. A. Stevens & Co., 29 and 31 Granby street.

Cigars.

M. Hofheimer, 207 and 209 Main street. (See advertisement).

Leading Clothing Establishments.

Wiginton & Bell, 168 Main street. (See advertisement).
F. A. Karn & Co., 166 Main street.
S. Hofflin, 164 Main street.
Odenhal & Vicar, 100 Church street, next to Main street.
M. Hohenfels (successor to Goldsmith Bros.), 88 Main street.
Jordan Bros., 124 Main street.
S. Frank & Co., 156 Main street.
Burk's, 112 and 114 Main street.

Coal and Wood.

Nottingham & Wrenn, 56 Main street. (See advertisement).
R. W. Santos & Co., 63 Water street.

Commission Houses (Cotton).

Vaughan & Barnes, McPhail's Wharf.
Royster & Strudwick, Room 10 Hare Building.
Rountree & Co., Rooms 5 and 6 Hare Building.
Eure, Farrar & Co., McPhail's Wharf.
J. W. Perry & Co., Tunis Wharf. (See advertisement).
Everett Bros., Gibson & Co., Room 9 Hare Building.
R. A. Dobie & Co., 2 and 4 Roanoke Square.
Battle, Bunn & Co.
Harrell Bros., 1 to 9 Commerce street.
Louis Hilliard & Co.
Etheridge & Fulgham, 15, 17, 19 and 21 Commerce street. (See advertisement).
J. C. Etheridge & Co., 5 Roanoke Dock. (See advertisement).
S. B. Harrell & Co.
S. J. Taylor, Higgins Wharf.

Commission Merchants (Produce).

Gresham & Ives, 11 and 13 Commerce street.
Etheridge & Fulgham, 15, 17, 19 and 21 Commerce street. (See advertisement).
J. W. Perry & Co., Tunis Wharf. (See advertisement).
J. C. Etheridge & Co., 5 Roanoke Dock. (See advertisement).
C. D. Jordan, 9 Roanoke Square.
S. B. Harrell & Co.

Commission Merchants (Pea-nuts).

Etheridge & Fulgham, 15, 17, 19 and 21 Commerce street. (See advertisement).

J. W. Perry & Co., Tunis Wharf. (See advertisement.
R. A. Dobie & Co., 2 and 4 Roanoke Square.
J. C. Etheridge & Co., 5 Roanoke Dock. (See advertisement).

Druggists, Wholesale and Retail.

Walke & Williams, cor. Water street and Roanoke Avenue. (See advertisement).
M. A. & C. A. Santos, 5 Bank street. (See advertisement).
John W. Burrow, head of Market Square.
Dr. D. C. Cannon's Pharmacy, 210 Butte street.
W. F. Phillips, 216 Main street, opposite Purcell House.
Benjamin F. Cason, Jr., & Co., 317 Church street, cor. Wood.

Dry Goods.

Harman R. Anderson, 202 Main street.
E. B. Blamire, 146 Main street.
Peter Smith, 144 Main street.

Engines and Boilers.

C. W. Pettit, 280–286 Water street. (Manufacturers).
George W. Duvall & Co., Water Street. (Manufacturers).
Mayer & Co., 4 and 6 Market Square. (Dealers and Agents).
E. V. White & Co., 12 Commercial Row. (Dealers and Agents). See advertisement.
Joseph J. McIntyre, 60 Roanoke Avenue. (Agent). See advertisement.

Fence (Farm, Garden and Ornamental).

O. M. Styron, 84 Union street.

Fertilizers.

R. A. Dobie & Co., the L. & R., 2 and 4 Roanoke Dock.
J. W. Perry & Co., Tunis Wharf.

Furniture, Carpets, &c.

Ames & Stevens, cor. Main and Granby streets. (See advertisement).
F. P. McIntyre, 208 Main street.
W. K. Allen, 153 Church street.

Grocers (Wholesale).

Washington Taylor, 14, 16 and 18 Commerce street.
T. A. Williams & Co., cor. Commerce and Elizabeth streets. (See advertisement).
W. F. Allen & Co., 99 Water street.
Etheridge & Moore, 77 Water street.

Hardware.

Mayer & Co., 4 and 6 Market Square.
J. G. Womble & Son, 19 (east side) Market Square.
E. V. White & Co., 12 Commercial Row. (See advertisement).
W. R. Hudgins & Co., 35 Market Square.

Hatters.

William Stevens, 167 Main street.
Walter J. Simmons, 169 Main street.

Hides, Furs and Wool.

S. Marx, 19 Roanoke Dock.

Hotels (First-class).

Atlantic.
St. James, J. A. Kennedy, Proprietor.
New Purcell.

Ice.

Nottingham & Wrenn, 54 Main street.

Iron Foundries and Machine Shops.

Atlantic (W. A. Anderson, Proprietor), 206, 208 and 210 Water street.

Elizabeth (C. W. Pettit, Proprietor), 280–286 Water street.

Jewelry, Diamonds and Watches.

Chapman & Gale, 152 Main street.
S. R. Smith, 11 Bank street.

Junk, Scrap and Damaged Cotton.

Charles H. Hey, 138 and 140 Water street.

Liquors, Wines, Cordials, Bitters (Wholesale and Retail).

E. Vance, 28 Market Square.
John O'Connor, 13 Campbell's Wharf.
Hewlitt & Manning, 8 Bank street.

Marine Railways.

W. A. Graves, 209–223 Water street.

Merchant Tailors.

Carey & Shipp, 94 Main street.
Capps & Brimmer, 189 Main street.
S. Brown, 195 Main street.

Mill Supplies.

Mayer & Co., 4 and 6 Market Square.
E. V. White & Co., 12 Commercial Row. (See advertisement).
Joseph J. McIntyre, 60 Roanoke Avenue. (Manufacturer's Agent). See advertisement.

Oil Cloths, Rubber Boots, Shoes, &c.

Peter Turney, 1 Market Square.

Oils.

Mayer & Co., 4 and 6 Market Square.
E. V. White & Co., 12 Commercial Row.

C. A. Nash & Co., 8 West Market Square.
Luther Sheldon, 16 West Market Square.
Walke & Williams, cor. Water street and Roanoke Square.
Joseph J. McIntyre, 60 Roanoke Avenue. (Agent).

Produce and Fruit Dealers.

Williams Bros., 26 Roanoke Square.

Railroad and Steam-boat Supplies.

E. V. White & Co., 12 Commercial Row. (See advertisement).
Mayer & Co., 4 and 6 Market Square.
Joseph J. McIntyre, 60 Roanoke Avenue. (See advertisement).

Real Estate Dealers and Auctioneers.

Gardner & Fentress, 29 Bank street.
H. L. Page & Co.

Boot and Shoe Stores.

Henry Brandt, 31 Market Square.
D. Lowenburg Company.
George R. Whitehurst, 29 Market Square.

Soda, Sarsaparilla, Mineral Waters, &c.

Norfolk Bottling Company, 76 and 78 Church street.

Seed Growers and Merchants.

George Tait & Son, 7 Market Square.

Sash and Blinds.

C. A. Nash & Co., 8 West Market Square.
Luther Sheldon, 16 West Market Square.

Tea, Coffee and Sugar.

Great Atlantic and Pacific Tea Company, 39 Market Square.

Tobacco, Cigars, Snuff, &c. (Wholesale).
B. F. Baxter & Co., 76 Water street.

For additional names and addresses of Norfolk's leading business houses, see supplementary list of Norfolk's mercantile and manufacturing establishments and transportation lines.

THE Sound and River Cities of North Carolina.

PART FIRST.

I realize that any attempt at a description of the sound and river cities of the State of North Carolina with Wilmington, her metropolis, left out would look strikingly ludicrous. It is for this reason that I have ventured upon the following explanations:

It is my intention in the immediate future to describe all the coast, sound and river cities of the great North State in three parts, the first embracing those situated upon Albemarle Sound and its tributaries; the second upon Pamlico Sound and the waters which flow into it, and third, the cities, towns and forts on the Cape Fear river.

My reason for describing the following cities first is that they are contiguous to Norfolk and, as a consequence, the most fit to accompany the first part of this volume.

Tarboro, Greenville, Murfreesboro, and a number of other cities which are situated upon streams that find a navigable tide-water outlet by way of the Albemarle and Chesapeake or the Dismal Swamp canals, are left out for the same reason as that given in my conclusion to Norfolk—sickness in my family, which forced me to stay by the bedside when, under more favorable circumstances, I would have been engaged in perfecting this book., I can, however, assure my readers that I shall make a great endeavor to rectify all these shortcomings in the forthcoming work.

GEO. I. NOWITZKY.

ELIZABETH CITY, N. C.,

THE BELLE OF THE PASQUOTANK.

England's virgin queen, the petted, petulant and piquant Elizabeth, never, in the very zenith of her remarkably prosperous reign, looked prouder upon her throne than does the active little city so well situated upon the Pasquotank river which bears her name; and the subjects of the stern queen never, even in the dark hours when the white sails of the Spanish armada were found hovering near the sunken rocks of Edystone, were more ready to defend her possessions than the sons and daughters of "Sweet Bessie," as the citizens fondly call their favored city, are to defend the good name of the queen of the Pasquotank.

It is alleged that about the time Tom Moore threw his slurs at Norfolk

A BRITON

concluded to seek rest for his body, and probably from his creditors, and selected this little city for his haven. The people, thinking him a gentleman of culture and refinement, extended him many courtesies and he was a welcome guest everywhere, but he abused their hospitality and the citizens soon found it out; for a magazine published in London found its way to Elizabeth City containing an article from the pen of this gentleman upon American Civilization, and claiming that that of the white American was not much, if any, in advance of the red. This changed their attitude towards him; their former generous hospitality gave way to a stiff reserve; in fact, Elizabeth City can actually lay claim to a "boycott" years before Mr. Boycott of Ireland furnished name for this process of getting rid of an objectionable person. They had so little to do with him that they literally froze him out, and so thoroughly convinced him that he was not wanted that when a brigantine dropped down the Pasquotank and upon her departure took with her (to the great delight of all the citizens) this unfortunate man from "perfidious Albion" the following oft-quoted lines, which proclaim to the world the marvelous jumping power of Pasquotank bull-frogs, were, it is said, first brought forth to reinforce the epigrammatic literature of the world:

"He came to the banks
  Of the Pasquotank,
Where the bull-frogs jump
  From bank to bank."

Full of conceit
  And pernicious ire,
A scoundrel at heart,
  An unmitigated liar.

When he left, the frogs
  On both the banks
Croaked themselves hoarse
  In chanting their thanks.

For fear that some of my readers may think that I am manufacturing history, I wish to state that I have heard several versions as to the origin of the first verse appertaining to the frogs, which has become literally a household rhyme throughout the North State. '

My authority for the others, as well as the distinguished and extinguished visitor from England, is based upon the following, which I consider reliable information:

While in conversation with a number of planters in Elizabeth City one of them, the oldest in the party, quoted this well-known rhyme, and upon my asking him if he could possibly tell when he first heard it he answered in the negative, at the same time inviting me to take a seat in his buggy, and, as an inducement to take a ride, assured me that he would bring me to the house of a lady who knew all about its history. I could scarcely repress a smile at the idea of making a trip in quest of such information, and told him that I hardly thought its history of sufficient consequence to make such a special effort to find. But the old gentleman insisted and held out more inducements. He informed me that the old lady was a relative of his; that she was the possessor of a number of old relics, pictures and so on, some of them belonging to the Colonial period, and that she wanted some expert to judge their value, as she wished to dispose of them.

All philosophers agree, at least those who have agreed to give the subject any thought, that we are all more or less vain, and I presume I am no exception to this philosophic ruling. To be called an expert was very agreeable, and I evidently thought that the compliment should be rewarded for I took a seat in the buggy and in a short time after was introduced to a lady whose head was whitened by the frosts of seventy winters; from her I gleamed sufficient information to justify what I have said about the Englishman's visit to the Pasquotank; and as to the rhyme she informed me that when a child she had heard it often, and although she retained the first two lines she could only recall that one of the others in the next couplet wound up with the rather uncomplimentary but expressive word—liar, while the concluding lines insisted that even the bullfrogs held a jubilee at the unfortunate's departure. With this to guide me, I wrote the lines as printed above, and after repeating them to her she said that they were nearly the same as the original. I then bade her good-bye, first, however, informing her where I thought she could sell her relics, and faithfully promising her that should I get into a controversy appertaining to jumping frogs and sarcastic Englishmen I would not mention her name, as she said she was too old to engage in a newspaper war.

This shows that the citizens of Elizabeth City have inherited this love of town and home, and whenever occasion demands it this innate love comes to the front. The last time that they felt as if they had sufficient grievance for general resentment was during the stirring days known by the citizens as the

The facts, as near as I can recall them, were as follows: When the Norfolk Southern Railroad was constructed only as far as Elizabeth City it bore the following modest title: The Norfolk and Elizabeth City Railroad; but after leaving the metropolis of the east side as a terminus, by continuing to Edenton, and thus finding herself increased in mileage and the two appendages which naturally follow—greater power and more usefulness—they concluded that they should be known by a stronger sounding name, the one selected being the present, which makes no mention of Elizabeth City. This provoked her citizens, and among them (far in the lead) was that stalwart champion of the sounds, or, as his friends fondly term him, "the great Democratic War-horse of Eastern Carolina"—Colonel Creecy, the editor of the *Economist*. So gallantly did he fight them in his excellent journal, and so thoroughly did the people appreciate his efforts, that they not only presented him with a gold-headed cane, but also gave his name to the prettiest park in the great North State.

The war is now happily over, for the railroad company, by furnishing a most excellent service and improving its magnificent water-front, has redeemed itself and once again has come into favor with the Colonel and the other citizens.

The city is divided into two parts which appear as distinct and unlike as if there was a hundred miles of space between them. This difference may not be as perceptible to the citizen, but is so marked that it is noticed by nearly every traveler. The lower is known as

THE WATER,

for the reason that it borders upon the river. Its leading streets are Water, Fearing and the lower end of Main. Water street is the shortest of the three, but it contains the heaviest mercantile establishments and most durable business buildings in the city.

MAIN STREET

begins at the river front, and any one viewing the Pasquotank from its wharf, I care not how much he has traveled, unless he has well studied and mapped in his mind the geographical features of the city and its spacious water approach, is apt to think that he is overlooking some bay having immediate connection with an ocean instead of standing on the banks of a river. The street is a pretty blending of business houses and residences; it is broad and well shaded by lofty elms. From the river front for two blocks it is lined with solid, well constructed brick business houses, then the elms begin and the street loses its city-like appearance, looking more like the main thoroughfare of the staid seat of a wealthy agricultural county. The effect is very pleasing as the visitor walks under the shade of the monster trees past the stately court-house, magnificent residences surrounded with green lawns, and the hospitable looking hotel. This handsome avenue, as I have before noted, has many changes in its great length, but there are two things it does not lose: its generous width and gracious shade.

The older or upper part of the city gives every evidence of having once been the most important, and

ROAD STREET,

its main thoroughfare, in spite of a number of dilapidated buildings, still looks substantial, and is also a pleasant street to walk through and reflect upon the "ups and downs" in the history of a city's streets, for this thoroughfare, judging by the appearance of its buildings, must have been the centre of trade before Water street, with its many handsome store-houses, was thought of. The greatest relic left to show its former grandeur is

AN OLD BANK,

built in the *ante-bellum* days, its somber Tuscan colonade supporting two platforms, one serving as a veranda for the second and the other for the attic story, which is faced by a huge fire-wall evidently made to take the place of the missing pediment. The building has a very peculiar, lonesome appearance, and if situated in California would readily be taken for a Jesuit Mission church.

A ramble through the streets of the city convinced me that the Pasquotank beauty will compare favorably, in the appearance and substantial nature of her buildings, with any city in North Carolina. The business houses are nearly all of brick, with well-designed fronts. The residences, it is true, are mainly of more perishable material, but there are two of brick which deserve special mention. One of them is on Main street, nearly opposite the court-house, and is owned by the

EDITOR OF A NEWSPAPER.

I am satisfied a smile expressing incredibility will play on the visage of any journalist that may read this, and I do not know that it will entirely disappear when I say that this gentleman is also a successful practicing attorney; but I am quite sure that it will vanish like feathers before a cyclone when I say that he owns a valuable ferry franchise, which enables outside Pasquotankers to come to Elizabeth City without following the example set by the frogs and jumping across the river.

The other is a more modern study and is owned by a prominent member of the North Carolina Bar, who is also one of the gentlemen who comprise the shell-fish commission of the bivalve-margined coast of the great North State.

The churches are all neat and well-cared-for, but I am sorry to say that there are only two that are built of enduring material : one belongs to the Episcopal and the other to the Methodist denomination. A neat tower, finished with battlements, is the special feature of the former and a Doric porch of the latter.

By far the handsomest structure in the city is

THE COURT-HOUSE.

It stands in the centre of a beautiful lawn which occupies a large square and is well inclosed with a neat iron railing. The building is the leading architectural feature of both town and judicial district. In fact, in exterior effect and surroundings it can well be classed as the finest judicial building in the Commonwealth, and in interior embellishments it is only surpassed by one (New Bern). It is built of brick, heavily trimmed with granite. Four rustic, stone-faced piers stand out in full relief from the first story of the building and hold a substantial granite platform, from which spring four columns, which, unfortunately, are the great defect of the building, on account of being severely plain when they should be fluted to correspond with the capitals, which are Corinthian, thus giving the impression that the building committee had exhausted their funds before the edifice was completed. These columns support the pediment, which contains a large granite slab with the date of construction (1882), and from the roof rises a well-designed and substantial cupalo, which contains a fine clock and bell, towering above all surroundings.

The Albemarle Hotel ranks among the largest hotel buildings in the State. Its imposing brick fronts, pierced by many windows, add much to the appearance of both Main and Broad streets.

Among the many attractions that Elizabeth City affords I found

THE FAIR GROUNDS,

which are well situated as well as very accessible, the main or grand entrance being a few feet from an improvised depot of the Norfolk Southern road. It has good buildings for exhibition purposes and ample stabling facilities, but its chief feature is its speeding track, which is rolled to such a nicety and kept in such perfect condition that it is criticised as being one of the "fastest" on the South Atlantic seaboard.

During a late visit to the city I concluded to take a drive to far-famed

CREECY PARK,

which I found contains about thirty acres of land and water, which nature has done a great deal for, and its primary attractions are being continually added to by well planned scenic, landscape and floral additions. It is well situated upon the banks of the majestic Pasquotank, which forms a most attractive and well sheltered harbor, and being a tidal stream it naturally affords every advantage for the location of bath-houses. A good depth of water a few feet out, reached by a well constructed wharf, gives superb facilities for the transportation of passengers brought by steam-boats and other craft.

Its present attractions are a great diversity in physical features with which nature first adorned it, and which consist of valley, glade and hill covered with an abundance of luxuriant grasses and shaded by thirty-two species of trees, and a remarkably well stocked fish-pond dotted with picturesque islands and bounded by cosy nooks and neat projecting headlands, while water-lilies dance on its mirrored surface, and rush and reed waft lazily with the breeze. Many birds, as if aware of the safety extended them by the land being posted, make the undergrowth their home and their cheery chirping, combined with the sighing of the trees and murmur of the waters, form a blending of pleasing sounds which it would be hard to duplicate.

Elizabeth City, in spite of the fact that the shores of the river do not abound in bluffs and other elevations, affords some beautiful scenery, and there is no better place to get a view of

THE BROAD PASQUOTANK

as it sweeps past its water-front than the doorway of the *Falcon* office. Being on the second floor, it has the proper elevation and the door acts as a frame, making it look like a magnificent painting by Raphael; that is, if Raphael had made the specialty of his life marine painting, and could imitate nature in her endless variety of color, the perpetual motion of the water and the glistening diamonds caused by the sun's reflection or the dimmer sparks for which the moon is responsible.

The deep basin of the ample harbor I could entirely overlook. To the left as well as the immediate front the shipping, although limited to steam-boats, schooners and sloops, was interesting, while to the right I could see busy factories and residences embowered in trees. A powerful marine glass, kindly lent me by a gentleman connected with the *Falcon*, reduced the ten miles of water to the fraction of one and showed me plainly the lonesome looking banks of the opposite shore, and revealed, to my surprise, a number of mills with large sweeping arms, taking advantage of the same wind that was propelling the many sail-boats through the intervening waters and forcing the smoke of an incoming revenue cutter to make a desperate endeavor to reach the sky.

THE MERCANTILE AND MANUFACTURING INTERESTS OF ELIZABETH CITY.

Present population, nearly 4,000; railroad, Norfolk Southern; steamboat lines, Norfolk Southern and Old Dominion; manufacturing, lumber, cotton seed oil, twine, carriages, brick, etc. Other interests, cotton and fish.

The following is a list of the majority of the leading and reliable business houses of Elizabeth City on January 1st, 1888:

Commission, Cotton, Produce, &c.
K. R. Newbold.

Drugs, Seeds, Cigars, &c.
Dr. W. W. Griggs.

Dry Goods, Clothing, &c.
Jacob Salomonsky.

Furniture (Wholesale and Retail).
C. W. Overman.

Groceries (Wholesale and Retail).
D. B. Bradford & Co.
J. B. Flora.
Harrison & Nash, cor. Water and Fearing streets.
J. P. Hughes, 29 and 30 Main street.

Groceries and Confectioneries.

C. W. Stevens, Main street, near Water.
C. A. Jackson, cor. Road and Fearing streets.

Hardware, Furniture, Windows and Doors.

John L. Sawyer.

Insurance.

George M. Scott.

Jeweler.

Louis Selig, Water street.
F. M. Cook.

Junk.

W. C. Glover, Fearing street.

Liquor (Wholesale and Retail).

J. B. Brocket.

Livery and Sale Stables.

A. L. Jones. (See advertisement).

Manufacturers.

C. C. Allen, Press, Re-press and Fancy Cornice Bricks.
Fowler's Net and Twine Factory.
J. F. Sanders, Carriages, Buggies, Road Carts. (See advertisement).
Joseph Salomonsky, Ginger Ale, Soda and Mineral Waters. (See advertisement).
G. W. Bell, Gun and Locksmith, Dealer in Sporting Goods.
Currier, Burroughs & Co., Sails, Awnings and Flags.
H. O. Hill, Tinware, Roofing and Guttering. Fearing street.
R. Madrin, Cabinet Maker and Undertaker.
J. W. T. Smith, Rubber Stamps and Painter.

Merchant Tailors.
Edward G. Schirmon, Fearing street.
Maurice Wescott, Main street.

Milk and Dairy Products.
C. B. Brothers, Road street.

Photographer.
H. Murphy, Road street.

Sewing Machines.
C. M. Alderson, Fearing street.

Undertaker.
John H. Ziegler. (See advertisement).

HERTFORD, N. C.

The first permanent settlement in the State of North Carolina was made at Durant's Neck on the Perquimans river, and in what is now known as Perquimans county. This I assert in spite of historians who persist in saying that the first settlement was made on the banks of the Roanoke river, when they should know that every *ante-Revolutionary* deed and record show that Albemarle Sound was formerly called Roanoke Sound, and that all transfers of real estate in the adjacent section were designated as being near the waters of the Roanoke, and that the undeniable fact stares them in the face that the first deed written and recorded in what is now the State of North Carolina was in this county and the land in question part of its area.

Perquimans is not, as a great many believe, the name of an Indian tribe who once inhabited this section, but means the land of pretty women. It was so named because of the many pretty Indian maidens that once inhabited this section; and every one who has been favored with a look at the fair faces of the fairer complexioned ladies that inhabit this same locality at the present time will readily admit that the name of the county should not be changed. It is also written that the Yeopim tribe of Indians, whose headquarters were less than a mile from the court-house, were as much noted for their intelligence as the maidens were for their beauty, and I am happy to bear witness to the fact that the male population have held their own as well as the female, for this little village of seven hundred population has actually for several years furnished the member of Congress for this Congressional District, containing one hundred and fifty-four thousand inhabitants, and at the same time the Solicitor. They are eloquent Tom Skinner and logical Jack Blount.

And this is not all, for when the State concluded to organize a college to teach the rising generation how best to tickle the soil for a crop, they naturally looked about for a superintendent, and when their eyes rested upon the map of Perquimans county they looked no further, but immediately made a requisition upon Hertford, and Mr. J. Skinner was brought to the front.

The majority of people evidently believe that there is very little to be seen in Hertford; and the most studious and observing commercial traveler shares in this belief.

As for myself, I certainly had no idea that there was so much to interest within its boundaries until I strolled forth in quest of subject-matter for its part in these pages.

Hertford being a county-seat, I naturally first walked to the

COURT-HOUSE,

a substantial brick structure, which stands in the centre of a grassy, elm-shaded lot that covers an entire block. It was built during the war of 1812, and in the Register's office I was shown the record of the oldest deed in the State. It was originally made out in 1661 and registered in 1716. It deeded to George Durant a large tract of land at what is now known as Durant's Neck. Kilcacanew, king of the Yeopim Indians, made the transfer, as his name, further guaranteed by his red majesty's royal seal (which consisted of a very poor drawing of a bow and arrow in very black ink), attested.

After feasting my eyes for some time on the *fac-simile* of the artistic work of the dusky king of the Yeopims, and looking at more musty records, I strolled further down Main street to the Episcopal church, which is an old wooden shed that did not repay my visit, but in the church-yard that surrounds it and runs back to where the bank slopes towards the Perquimans I found considerable to interest me. The handsomely embellished monument which is erected over the grave of Mrs. Elizabeth Ann Bunch is a very nicely executed study, and the stone to the memory of Mary Catherine, the infant daughter of Dr. N. G. Skinner, shows that, in the hands of a proper artist, even a small stone can become a gem.

After leaving this little grave-yard, which is also situated on Main street, I concluded to walk up to Church street and look at the architectural pride of the village,

THE BAPTIST CHURCH.

It stands upon a nicely turfed, artistical mound, created for that purpose. It is built of brick and has a solid, substantial appearance, which justifies what is claimed for it—that it is the best building in the county.

At the back of this edifice and the extreme end of the mound I found, to my surprise, two treasures in the form of storied marble. I say surprise, because I have often visited Hertford and never heard of their existence before. One of these monuments (that erected to the memory of Mrs. Mary Felton) would attract attention anywhere. It is in the decorated Gothic style, upon a high base formed of three receding blocks of marble upon which rest four handsomely capped columns which support a canopy, and from its leaf-decorated roof springs a Gothic steeple. Under this canopy is the figure of a woman in classic robes resting upon an urn which stands upon a pedestal. The pose of the statue is easy and life-like, and the monument, as a whole, ranks among the best in the State. The other memorial stands by its side and does not rank with the one just described as a work of art, but is so much over the average marble that decorates the country church-yards that it would readily attract attention. It is composed, first, of a solid granite base; upon this stands the body of the monument, composed of four parts, all differently embellished without destroying the general harmony; then an obelisk capped by a draped urn, and covered with a stone, upon which stands that well-known emblem of love, the dove, cut in spotless marble. They are enclosed with an appropriate iron railing with lambs resting under weeping willows for panels. Why these monuments are thus literally secreted is more than I can see, and why the indications of a superior taste, a love of art among the people, and that art lovingly placed by affectionate hands over the graves of deceased relatives, should be thus hidden from observation is more than I can explain. Some may account for it by saying that it would not be in good taste, or that it would be considered ostentatious to make a display of marble made to commemorate the lives of the dead. But if that is the case, what was the object in cutting them in the first place? Why should the skill of the artist be invoked to get them to such marvelous perfection unless they were intended to be seen? Further, does it not show that the sleepers who silently repose under their shadows were loved and appreciated? Then why cut day and date and obituaries upon enduring stone and then hide them? It may be right, but it seems very inconsistent.

This little town, like the majority of the cities of Eastern North Carolina, has the advantage of railroad as well as water transportation, as the Norfolk Southern road brings its trains to one end of the corporation and the deep Perquimans river gives excellent wharfage at the other.

The following is a classified list of the leading business houses of Hertford on January 1st, 1888:

Drugs, Paints, Oils.

Dr. J. H. McMullen.

Fire and Life Insurance.

George M. Newby.
A. Arps.

General Merchandise.

T. B. Blanchard & Bro.
W. T. McMullen & Co.
Norman Bros.
W. R. Shannonhouse.
Tobias Baker.

Livery, Sale and Trade Stables.

M. H. White.
T. S. White.

Manufacturers.

Toms & McMullen, Carriages, Wagons and Carts.
J. M. Whedbee, Lumber and Flour.

School.

Hertford High, A. M. Simmons, A. B., Principal.

Undertakers.

W. F. Stokes, Undertaker and Contractor.
W. H. Vaughan, Undertaker and Coach-maker.

Wells (Artesian and others).

T. D. Saunders.

EDENTON,

THE GEM OF THE SOUNDS.

NOTE.—I am satisfied that the following description of Edenton is familiar to the majority of North Carolinians, as I originally wrote it for the *News and Observer*, Raleigh, and being published in that widely circulated journal and copied by a number of other State papers, it is natural to suppose that it was very generally read. My reason for inserting it here is that no material changes have taken place since, and, as a consequence, it fills the bill as well as any description that I could give to-day of North Carolina's most picturesque city:

For her southern boundary, one of the loveliest sheets of water on the South Atlantic coast; for her western, a sparkling, limpid creek, named in honor of England's stern queen, Elizabeth—a creek whose banks abound in sylvan dells and fairy-like nooks, and on whose lazy, laughing waters lilies dance in great profusion; for her eastern, another sparkling stream, named after another of England's rulers—Queen Ann—which pours its accumulation of waters by way of pretty Edenton Bay, to mix with the sterner waves of Albemarle Sound. Thus favorably situated, you will find Edenton, the county-seat of Chowan county, a little city rich in her history, wealthy in the retention of her

OLD LANDMARKS,

and doubly fortunate in her pastoral beauty and picturesque glimpses of land and water, for from her "city wharf" the eye of the spectator overlooks ten miles of

Albemarle's silver-capped waves, as it rests upon the panorama of blue hills which form the opposite shore, and when he faces about to gain an inland vista he is rewarded with an uninterrupted view of the finest avenue in the State, for Main street has been laid out so generously that it is wide enough to permit three lines of majestic elms to grow, and these have done much toward making the town "famous." These trees are led by one which is more noticeable by day and doubly attractive by night, for it serves as a light-house by which the mariner can with safety navigate his bark into this favored port, and as he walks up the shaded "boulevard" he is not disappointed, for one block brings him to

EDEN PALACE,

a quaint-looking structure which was framed in England and erected upon its present site in 1758. Opposite this monument of another century stands another old structure, in which it is claimed that the ladies of Colonial Edenton gathered and resolved not to drink another cup of tea until the tax imposed by Great Britain should be repealed. From here he passes a number of fairly constructed modern business houses and then a number of pretty cottages. Here he is once more confronted by a relic of another age. This time it is

"OLD ST. PAUL'S" CHURCH,

the venerable walls of which are constructed of brick imported from England many years before the war for independence. This noble edifice is situated in the centre of a pretty church-yard, in which repose some of the once leading men and women of the State; and that they were loved by those that knew them best is well attested by the many beautiful and attractive monuments that mark their last resting-place.

It is with regret that the stranger turns away from this street of quiet beauty, but there is much more to been seen in this museum-like little city, and prominent among the sights stands

THE OLD COURT-HOUSE.

This grand old landmark, which has served as a day beacon for the mariner for over a hundred years, not only contains, I am informed, the oldest Masonic lodge-room in the State, but also the identical chair occupied by our illustrious first President when Grand Master. Even to the stranger not acquainted with its history this building has anything but a commonplace appearance; for its present elevation, crowned by a well proportioned cupola, has often been pronounced by competent judges an architectural study worthy of the place and surroundings; but to him who realizes that it was used both as a provincial and State capitol building it is a study of still more interest.

In front of this, North Carolina's most historic building, is the square laid out by the wise forefathers who planned this ideal village for a "public green." There are no studied walks, classic statuary, or murmuring fountains in this little park, but the grass looks a brighter green than that further inland, and an air of quiet and peace prevails which readily turns one into

A DAY-DREAMER,

and as he looks out upon the magnificent stretch of water which lies at his feet, he cannot help but think that he is standing upon the "stretch" where the ancient fishermen "were wont" to repair their nets, and as the shades of eve dim the outlines of the distant hills and nearer court-house, fantastic shapes which assume the forms of people of another age seem to arise, and he can easily imagine that he has drifted back to the powdered wigs and knee-breeches of the Colonial age.

This town is also happy in her hotel accommodations, the tourist having the choice of two well-kept taverns. The oldest is known as the Woodward House, and enjoys the enviable reputation of having been an inn since 1750, and the still more enviable reputation of having always been well-kept. The other hotel, known as the Bay View, is a more modern structure, but covers every inch of the site of the Kings Arms, an ancient tavern of *ante*-Revolutionary reputation.

Thus beautifully situated between her two queenly named creeks, Edenton, as calmly as

HER PEERLESS BAY

in fair weather, rolls year after year into the immeasurable depth of time, with nothing to disturb her equanimity except when the death of some distinguished or loved citizen is announced. But this only causes a gentle ripple, for the religious and good people content themselves by saying, "It is as He who made us all willed it." The body with solemn ceremony is entombed, and the city of the dead, so solemnly situated around the staunch walls of "old St. Paul's" church, increases at the expense of living Edenton.

Some may say that it is too bad that capital and enterprise do not find their way into its time-honored boundaries, but I think in this case the hand of the usual improvement would be unfortunate, for what modern store-house placed on its site could cope in interest or attraction for the stranger with the cupola-capped palace of Royal Governor Eden? What stately court-house, built since its erection, could we have the same affection for as

THE OLD PILE

from whose doorway the stentorian voices of court-criers have been heard for a hundred years as they summoned jurors and witnesses before judges too numerous to mention? And lastly, what modern ecclesiastical structure could compare with St. Paul's as it stands; its aged walls colored "as time only can color," like a sentinel over the dead, and giving consolation to the living?

For these reasons I reiterate that what would improve this place, in the general acceptation of the term, would be a misfortune to both State and nation. Then let us hope that the moss-covered roofs and noble elms will long survive, and that in the future, as in the past, the very brightest star in North Carolina's brilliant constellation of historic towns and cities will be Edenton, the gem of the sounds.

EDENTON'S BUSINESS INTERESTS AND BUSINESS MEN.

Population, about 1,600; leading business interests, mercantile and fishing; railroad, Norfolk Southern; steam-boat lines, Norfolk Southern Railroad Company's boat and the "Chowan" to Franklin, Va.

The following is a classified list of Edenton's most energetic and enterprising business establishments and leaders in their respective lines on January 1st, 1888:

Banker.
J. R. B. Hathaway.

Drugs.
Hooper & Co.
Dr. W. J. Leary.

Dentists (Surgical and Mechanical).
Dr. C. P. Bogart.

Dry Goods and Clothing.
L. Levy, Dillon Building.
O. Newman, Perkins' old stand.

Fish Shipping Establishments.
Shepard, Goodwin & Co.
W. D. Rea.
John C. Bond.
W. L. Arendell & Co.

General Merchandise.
J. E. Bonner.
E. B. Mitchell.

Groceries.
M. H. Dixon.
A. T. Bush.

Hotels.
Woodward House, John L. Rogerson.
Bay View, T. A. White, Proprietor.

Manufactories.

Baker & Son, Coach-makers.
C. M. Murden, Harness-maker and Saddler.

Shoes and Gentlemen's Furnishing Goods.

J. C. Sharp.

Undertakers.

C. M. Murden.
L. F. Ziegler, Undertaker and Cabinet-maker.

PLYMOUTH, N. C.,

THE BATTLE-SCARRED TOWN OF THE ROANOKE.

There is no town or city in the United States that shows more scars of war than Plymouth, N. C. Every few steps within the business portion brought me to excavations and low stone walls which but too plainly show that they were formerly cellars and foundations to buildings that have passed into smoke, ashes and history. Its war record is indeed strange. Being considered a great strategic point by the Federals as well as the Confederates, every effort was made by them to capture it; as a consequence, it was at different times in the hands of the armies and navies of both the contending governments, and, as if that was not sufficient, when they were gone it was robbed by desperate Buffaloes and plundered by rollicking Guerillas.

It was here that a Federal naval lieutenant, accompanied by a number of desperate men, shattered the hopes of this section of the Confederacy by shattering the iron sides of the Confederate ram Albemarle, through the agency of a powerful torpedo, while she was quietly lying at the wharf to be in readiness to keep back the Federal fleet, and sending her to the bottom of the Roanoke, thus throwing that historic stream open to the invaders.

Under these trying circumstances, it is not surprising to hear that when the dark clouds of civil strife were dispelled and ever welcome peace was making every effort to unite the severed cords of fraternity which once bound and united us as a nation, that when his searching rays fell upon the banks of the winding Roanoke, he found where beautiful Plymouth once stood nothing but ghostly-looking brick chimneys and stone foundations which could not burn. It was so thoroughly ruined and devastated that only one structure remained —the unfinished Episcopal church. But no armies or fires could rob her of what nature gave her—her splendid situation for trade and manufacture. Nearly two thousand people, at the present time, find occupation and pleasant homes in this, the county-seat of Washington county.

GRACE EPISCOPAL CHURCH

is the only notable building in the town. It is of the early English type and unlike any other structure in the State; it has a decidedly aged appearance and would easily be mistaken for one of the venerable ecclesiastic edifices built by the Established Church before the Revolution. This, however, is not the case, for the corner-stone was laid in 1860, and as the conflict between the

States commenced that year it stood unfinished until the war was over. In the venerable church-yard that surrounds this structure, and antedates it by many years, are a number of quaint tombstones, and on the south end is a very heavy and well constructed granite vault worthy of notice.

The town is full of legends of

BURIED WEALTH.

Black Beard, the notorious pirate who made Plymouth a frequent resort, it was generally presumed, buried a great deal of his quickly acquired wealth within the limits of the town to keep it from being as quickly lost; and about the time that everybody concluded it was buried beyond all hopes of being found the Civil War came, and with it not alone the army, but also more reports of secreted treasures. Among the many stories of this nature, and the one most generally believed, is that a sutler who sold the Federal army very few goods for a great deal of money, fearing that the soldiers would sometime raid his premises, concluded to secrete his gains in the quaint old grave-yard, and before he found use for it or thought it wise to recover it, he was taken sick, died and was also consigned to a grave-yard. This led to one of the most stirring episodes connected with the history of this historic town. Two gentlemen, well known as able jurists and statesmen, concluded that they had discovered a clue to the whereabouts of the sutler's buried treasure, and naturally concluding that it was doing no good where it was, and brought to light might be made useful, with the assistance of a mate of a steam-boat which made Plymouth one of its landings, organized themselves into an expedition for the special purpose of unearthing this treasure, which they had reason to believe was buried in a part of Grace church-yard which at that time was not used for cemetery purposes. The night selected was dark and dismal, and as they walked down to this resting-place of the dead and alleged safe of the sutler, the only way they could keep up their spirits was by reflecting what a vast amount of good the money, now useless, would do by relieving the wants of the poor and distressed, and educating worthy fatherless children; and, to their credit, be it said, that each made a firm resolve that half of the restored wealth should be used for these purposes. No time was lost, for as soon as they reached the little cemetery the digging commenced. It must have been a weird scene; the light (all that could be forced from an ordinary stable lantern) had just sufficient illuminating power to shed a faint, ghastly glimmer on the time-honored tombstones and vaults, a fitting one, however, to act as an accompaniment to the dull but continued thuds of the pick. It is generally believed that the same dim substitute for the sun never had its rays forced back by the reflecting force of the sutler's hoarded gold. But this appears to be the only effort in which this party has ever been unsuccessful; for one of these gentlemen has been Governor of the great North State, is loved by all her people, and to-day worthily represents the greatest nation on earth (ours) at an imperial court, vested with unlimited power, as the rank Minister Plenipotentiary signifies. The other is also well loved and trusted by the people, for having represented his District in Congress once, his constituents urged him to accept the position again, and his return by an overwhelming majority proved his popularity. As for the mate, the last time I heard of him he was still treading the deck of a steamer that displaces the waters of Chesapeake Bay, the Albemarle and Chesapeake Canal and legendary Roanoke river.

PLYMOUTH'S BUSINESS AND BUSINESS MEN.

Transportation, Norfolk Southern Railroad Company's steam-boats, Cashie Navigation Company and the "Chowan"; leading interests, lumber, manufacturing, fishing and mercantile.

The following list embraces Plymouth's most energetic and enterprising business houses on January 1st, 1888:

Druggists and Pharmacists.
B. F. Butler.
Robertson & Bryan.

Dentist.
A. Mathews, D. D. S.

General Merchandise.
Sherwood & Newberry.
E. A. Carter & Co.
M. J. Norman & Co.
M. J. Bunch.

Livery and Sale Stables.
Joseph Skittletharpe.
Samuel Baynor.

Manufactories.
Boyle & Lehman, Lumber.
Perry Machine Works.
H. Peal, Carriage.
George R. Bateman, Carriage and Coach.

WINDSOR, N. C.

Windsor, the county-seat of Bertie county, contains about eight hundred inhabitants, and is situated at the head of navigation of the Cashie, a very narrow, very crooked, but very deep tributary of the Roanoke. It was founded in 1722, the site being given by an enterprising planter with the stipulation that it should "forever be used as a town."

The main thoroughfare, King street, is well shaded by large elms, which form so perfect an arch that the sun has little chance to throw her rays upon any part of it. It is pleasant to stand upon the deck of the steamer "Bertie" on a spring morning and look through this green tunnel nearly a mile in length. One line of steamers, the Cashie Navigation Company, bring passengers and freight to her wharf daily; and a number of other steam-boats that make irregular trips tie up at her landings.

THE NEW COURT-HOUSE

now under construction, the material brick and stone, promises to be a structure worthy of both town and county. It replaces a building that antedated the Revolution, and standing in a well-shaded square will, when completed, make a handsome appearance.

The following are Windsor's principal business houses:

General Merchandise.
J. P. Rascoe & Son.
J. B. Nichols.
R. C. Razemore.

Hardware and Agricultural Implements.
J. J. Jacocks.

Jeweler, Watchmaker and Photographer.
C. T. Harden.

Manufactories.
P. Rascoe, Hubs, Spokes, Sawed Lumber, &c.
R. W. Goode & Son, Lumber.
R. H. Small, Lumberman.
E. S. Dail, Carriage, Wagon, and Undertaker.

Transportation Line.
Cashie Steam Navigation Company.

GATESVILLE, N. C.

The merchants of Gatesville, the county-seat of Gates county, are no longer compelled to haul their goods over the three miles of "corduroy" which is the only road that connects it with Gates Landing or the Chowan river, and is very generally conceded the worst piece of road in America. for more involuntary tall and lofty tumbling has been done upon it, and more swearing indulged in by passengers who have been so unfortunate as to be compelled to take it, than any other three miles in the world. But, as I have before stated, it is no longer necessary for the patient and long-suffering merchants of Gatesville to have their crockery, glassware and other easily broken merchandise smashed into shapeless fragments, for a deep navigable creek which forms one of the boundaries of the town has its waters stirred up several times a week by the propellers of freight-carrying steam-boats.

The material improvements of the town consist first of a neat Episcopal church surrounded by a well-shaded yard. In this connection, I will say that there are two more churches, the Baptist and Methodist, both well supported, but the buildings are of wood. The next is the solid, substantial court-house of brick faced with granite, built in 1863. Its doorway is shaded by two lofty elms, and in a little square in front stands the public well, always abundant in cool water. It looks exceedingly refreshing on a warm court day to see its long sweep continually going up in the air, its reach down into the well, and then reverse and come forth with the oaken bucket filled and running over with the purest of beverages, Nature's great invigorator—limpid, sparkling water.

Gatesville contains about 300 inhabitants, and the following list gives its leading business houses on January 1st, 1888:

Drugs, Seeds, Cigars, &c.

C. D. Bell, M. D.
A. R. Roberts.

SOUND AND RIVER CITIES OF N. C.

General Merchandise.

W. R. Hayes & Co.
R. B. G. Cowper.
T. E. Cross.
R. M. Riddick.
C. W. Cross & Co.

Hotel and Livery.

United States, T. E. Hayes, Proprietor.

Manufactories.

W. H. Edwards, Carriages, Wagons, Carts, and Undertaking.
W. H. Standin, Carriages, Buggies, Carts, and Undertaking.

Real Estate.

John Brady.

WINTON, N. C.

Wide, straight and well laid out are the streets of Winton. They cross at right angles and are well situated upon an elevated plain, high and dry above the Chowan river. This plateau being perfectly level and easily drained, makes a magnificent town site. The present population is about 500. Its main street is nearly a hundred feet wide, and its present buildings of note are a well designed court-house, consisting of a two-story brick centre crowned by a cupola and flanked by two wings, the most picturesque as well as substantial looking jail in Eastern North Carolina, a brick Masonic Hall, stuccoed to imitate stone, and a fine residence of the same material.

The following is a list of the leading business men of Winton on January 1st, 1888:

General Merchandise.

Shaw Bros.
Mathews & Bro.
Mitchell & Askew.
E. W. Mitchell.

Insurance (Fire, Marine, Life and Live Stock).

W. J. Smith, Agent.

Real Estate Brokers.

Anderson & Aumach.

PART SECOND.

NEW BERN,

THE ELM-SHADED CITY OF THE NEUSE.

In rugged, hilly Person county, near the Virginia border, the Neuse under another name first leaves mother earth for its race to the sea. After gaining a little strength he thinks he is strong enough to smoke his first cigar, pipe, or both, as he takes a straight course for tobacco-famed Durham county, and, after crossing it collects all the strength, in the form of tributaries, that he can in Wake, Johnston, Wayne, Lenoir and Craven to the point where he stands out boldly as one of the leading figures in this descriptive sketch. For one hundred miles, as near as careful calculation can make it, the Trent, born in fair Duplin, forces its way like an enamored maiden through Jones county, and after reaching Craven at the point before mentioned, as if tired of being single, makes all possible haste to throw herself into the strong embraces of the more powerful Neuse.

On the land washed by these streams at their meeting, as if intended for an eternal witness of this union, and to see that nothing shall them ever sever, stands fair, elm-shaded New Bern, which was founded in 1710 by that mysterious figure in North Carolina's early history,

CAVALIER DE GRAFFENREID,

who, getting tired of such simple amusements as courting the Queen of England and other ladies, fighting duels and waltzing giddily over the waxed floors of London's palaces, left all the luxuries of Queen Ann's British Court for the forests and all the privations that awaited him in the wilds of North America. After being captured by Indians and sentenced to death he was released by posing as a king, the Indians evidently having more respect for royalty than Nihilists have for Czars.

This episode, coupled with some minor troubles, was sufficient to show the gallant Baron that life was attended (at that time) with more pleasure in Europe than America, for he retraced his course and left "New Bern," North Carolina, for his native city, old "Bern," in the mountains of Switzerland.

Nearly all

THE STREETS OF NEW BERN

cross at right angles and, on account of the great variety of architectural styles invoked to shape its buildings, the beautiful grounds that surround its dwellings, the well-shaded and well-cared-for roadways (which form a splendid combination of shelled drives), interest and delight the stranger.

The two principal business streets are Middle and Pollock. The first gives frontage on its lower end to prominent business houses and the upper to fine residences, while Pollock has for its centre some of the leading business houses of the city, and the ends are faced with neat dwellings. But, to me, the street to recall the past and give all the links in   .

NEW BERN'S CHAIN OF TIME

is Front. It commences at the east, amid a number of busy, buzzing saw-mills, and then follows all the variations of the eccentric Neuse. At the corner of Union a number of old but substantial, solid brick structures are brought to view, which not only enable the stranger to form an idea of the homes of the leading town class in the South before the war between the States, but also show that she had good mechanics as well as great statesmen, merchants and planters in those days, for these buildings were put there to stay, and their present condition gives evidence that they did not disappoint their builders.

A short distance from here I found a pretty parkway, the land side bordered by handsome residences, surrounded by green lawns, trees and shrubs, while on the other flows the Neuse, which here is very broad, and the great length of the river plainly visible without any interruption (for, like the sea, it is here lost in space), combined with the projecting headlands clothed in verdure, and the peculiar color of the water, make a beautiful picture.

The shores of this pretty esplanade are kept from washing by a substantial sea-wall, and three lines of trees shade it. A few dollars well expended in rustic seats and other embellishments would make this one of the most beautiful spots in the eastern counties of the State.

A short walk from here (on Front, corner Middle) brought me to what may well be termed the greatest

ARCHITECTURAL CURIOSITY

in the South. It is formed of two of New Bern's oldest brick buildings (one has done duty as a jail), transformed into such a remarkable combination and blending of dormers, balconies, pinnacles, fantastic-looking tower, railings, human, griffin and dog heads as to make it a veritable architectural puzzle. No one knows what it is intended for, and the owner, evidently believing it nobody's business, has failed to enlighten them.

In reviewing the city's stateliest buildings I must give a leading place to

CRAVEN COUNTY COURT-HOUSE,

which is conceded by all to have the finest interior of any judicial structure in the State, and quite a number of the Judges who have seen the ninety-six that adorn the counties of the Commonwealth think its exterior also ranks first. It is indeed an imposing edifice of brick, stone and iron, covered with a many-colored slate mansard, and a large square tower with a place for a town clock adds greatly to the beauty of the structure. New Bern has

TWO CHURCHES

which are particularly noticeable. The Episcopal, which has a commanding situation and is surrounded by a large and well-cared-for church-yard, and faces on two of her best streets, is without a doubt the most imposing ecclesiastical structure in the sound districts of North Carolina. It is of brick, and its front elevation is relieved by an ornamental memorial porch, which, unfortunately, is too low to conform consistently with the main edifice; but its greatest feature is its tall, massive tower, from which springs a well proportioned steeple, which is surmounted by a metal crown that looks like gold in the sunshine, and can be seen by the mariner many miles away as he sails in from the sea.

The Baptist is the only other brick church in the city. It is in the English mediæval style, with heavy tower and battlements, and its substantial walls, with ivy clinging to them, do much towards beautifying Middle street.

The well-shaded campus of the

NEW BERN ACADEMY

has that attractive and cool appearance which is noticed about the grounds of Harvard and Yale, and the air about it seems just as much loaded with literature. The old, venerable building (which looks as if it might have been put there to enter into a contest against time with Tryon's palace), the new one with its Latin inscription, the many elms and green grass, all combine to produce this desired effect.

The most interesting building now standing in New Bern is one of the wings of

TRYON'S HISTORIC PALACE.

It is not remarkable on account of grandeur, ornamentation or size, but because it is the most historical structure in the State. Not only was it the palace of Royal Governor Tryon, but Washington used it for a stable, and after refusing to be reduced to ashes when a colored woman succeeded in burning the rest of the structure, its stalwart walls so firmly resisted the picks of Federal soldiers, who during the late war wanted to build chimneys out of its aged brick, that they concluded it would be cheaper to buy new ones.

The stranger who stands and looks at this relic of the past should realize that within its modest walls has been held the beautiful service of the Episcopal Church; that more than a hundred years back its walls echoed with the merry laughter of ladies with powdered wigs as they waltzed with gentlemen in knee-breeches over its floors; that many times the cheery voices of school-boys have been heard within its confines, repeating lessons which were to assist them in shaping their future; and the neighing of horses belonging to the Continental army. But the exterior appearance of Tryon's great palace was unquestionably exaggerated. To read the descriptions of that date we would expect a creation equal to Solomon's Temple and surpassing the existing cathedrals of Europe; but it was without doubt the finest building in the British North American colonies at the close of the Revolutionary war, and the inhabitants can well be pardoned for their enthusiasm when we realize that in that early period in our nation's history the log-cabin was, to a great extent, the residence, and the steepled framed church a grand realization.

As I promised in my preface, I have studiously avoided mentioning individual interests at the expense of public description, but when private enterprise has adorned a city with its greatest building the description is not alone pardonable, but necessary, for as much as Tryon's gubernatorial palace stood ahead of the log-cabin architecture of that period just as far has

THE TOURIST'S PALACE, "THE ALBERT,"

distanced all the hotel buildings in architecture, decorating and furnishing that have been created, prior to its erection, in the sound and river districts of North Carolina. Just as much as Tryon's great palace was the boast of New Bern and New Bernians in the *ante*-Revolutionary period just as much is the Hotel Albert, or, as some fondly call it, the Royal Albert, their sensation at the present day. The exterior, although a very neat study in pressed brick, with a noble vestibule flanked with niches, and a commanding tower, is no comparison to the interior, which is a happy combination of pretty vistas, stained glass with its cheering tints, and other effects which impress themselves with every step. Its public rooms are resplendent with sweeping mirrors, and the furniture and carpets show taste and its outgrowth— harmony in color. But the architect and decorator appear to have concentrated their genius upon the diningroom, which is handsomely decorated, gold-framed panels being the leading effect. The tower, like everything else about this structure, bears the impress of solidity and elegance, and is indeed a happy finish to this well-designed edifice. Every step that leads to it is carpeted, and as much attention has been paid in the design and finish of everything, from floor to ceiling, as if it was intended for the permanent *boudoir* of a lady instead of a simple outlook (and for that matter, in-look), for upon gaining access to this aerial, crystal-like point of observation the stranger will find that he has the advantage of two views, an interior as well as exterior, as a well-designed railing, which looks so substantial that it inspires the most timid with confidence, stands between him and a plunge of fifty feet. To look down this shaft by peeping over the railing is a temptation which few can resist before feasting their eyes upon the magnificent panorama that awaits their gaze. To the east is the dense green forest of the Pamlico shore, washed by the waters of the tireless Neuse; to the north, the city's roofs, the sky-line broken by the steeple-capped tower of Christ Episcopal church with

ITS GLISTENING CROWN,

which in the golden sunlight gives forth rays that can easily be construed as meaning "Peace on earth, good-will to all," and when the weather looks forbidding and dark clouds form over the city, as if eager for the coming storm, its great height and conspicuous position seemingly assures and says: "There is a crown beyond the grave." The many-colored slate mansard of the court-house, the stern-looking battlements which are placed upon the highest elevation of the Baptist church, the many-storied tower of the Presbyterian, and the outline of the steeple under whose shadow the Methodists worship. To the west, the deep-green trees which have made New Bern famous, and to the south, the grandest view of all. On the right is the Trent shimmering in the sunlight and gently, seemingly reluctantly, gliding towards the mightier Neuse in order to pay him homage and acknowledge that she is only a tributary; to the immediate front, first, many substantial business houses, then the wharves lined with shipping; a number of schooners, sloops, tugs, a Revenue cutter, anchored mid-stream, and other craft will next attract attention, and then James City, upon the opposite shore, with its connecting railroad bridge, will centre the eye. But to the left, the visitor must look for the grandest realization of this superb view. It is the meeting of the waters of the stern Neuse with those of the gentler Trent, for it is here that the latter stream loses its identity, and the two combined form the grand estuary which rolls on to the sea.

THE TWO GREAT CEMETERIES

of New Bern are probably better known than any other in either of the Carolinas, with the exception of that solemn Moravian "cedar walk" between Salem and Winston, and celebrated "Magnolia" at Charleston, with its huge oaks, their branches decorated with waving masses of Spanish moss.

CEDAR GROVE CEMETERY

has distinct features which make it unlike any other in the State, and I doubt if it has anything that borders on a reproduction in the United States; these features are the stone wall which encloses it and the main gateway. The first thing upon approaching this resting-place of the dead that attracts the stranger's eye is this quaint wall which divides it from life and the living. It is built of a curious formation peculiar to New Bern and vicinity, and known as Shell Rock; it has a time-colored and venerable appearance which makes it all the better adapted for the purpose. Of all the stone I have ever seen, none is more appropriate; of all the walls that enclose the dead, none are better designed.

THE WEEPING ARCH,

the name by which the gateway is known, being native to the soil, in fact of it (for it is fashioned out of the same stone), as if in sympathy with the grief-stricken relatives, weeps as the funeral procession goes under it. I am not writing at random, but giving facts, undeniable facts; for this rock being porous, when it rains it retains a considerable quantity of the water and permits it to gradually drop down, thus earning its name.

Once inside of this sacred enclosure, you realize that you are in a cemetery that many years have made interesting. Time-eaten tombstones of ancient patterns, aged tombs covered with large slabs containing quaint inscriptions, and moss-grown vaults, are intermingled with modern and costly monuments of glistening, polished granite and spotless marble.

This is also historical as well as sacred ground, for most active participants in five wars rest here: heroes that followed Washington through the snow at Valley Forge during the Revolution which established us as a nation, defenders who disputed every foot of ground with British invaders during the war of 1812, men who fought with Andrew Jackson in Florida and convinced Osceola and the Seminoles that the white man was destined to rule America, volunteers who fought with Taylor at Buena Vista or followed the fortunes of Scott from Vera Cruz to the very halls of Montezuma, and last, but not by any means least, the

SOLDIERS OF THE CONFEDERACY,

for in its very centre and most conspicuous spot stands the Confederate monument. It represents the heroic figure of a soldier who wore the gray, cut in immaculate marble and firmly standing upon a high and massive pedestal. The pose is dignified, the expression grand, and the entire work reflects great credit upon the people that had it erected and the artist who created such a lifelike reproduction. Nearly a hundred soldiers find final repose from the turmoil of war and life's many sorrows under its shadow.

The many phases of civil life are also well represented, for here lie the remains of those eminent statesmen and jurists, scholarly, logical and rhetorical William Gaston, and that giant in debate, John Stanley; the two Governor Spaights; Joseph H. Flanner, the European agent of the Confederacy; Dr. Barker, the eminent phrenologist; Mrs. Mary Bayard Clarke, who has enriched literature with many gems in both poetry and prose; Mrs. Hancock, whose poems have so many times cheered the despondent and consoled the sick, and many other men and women who gained distinction in various spheres of life now sleep "the eternal sleep" in this cedar-shaded, hallowed rest.

It was on a pleasant summer's Sunday evening, about five P. M. (during my last visit to New Bern), that I ordered a buggy, and after making enquiries as to the road, headed the horse toward the

NATIONAL CEMETERY.

It was a very lonesome drive, but its very lonesomeness possessed a charm that the hum of active business and the bustle of a much-used road would have dispelled. Not a single soul did I meet after crossing the railroad track, which, I presume, marks the city's line, for beyond it I observed only one solitary house, and that appeared uninhabited; as a consequence, I can fairly say that nothing about me appeared to have life except the horse I was driving and the grand old Neuse, whose silvered surface looked stern and melancholy.

It was a magnificent evening to visit a cemetery, everything being in its favor: the quiet that accompanies the day of worship in a Christian community was perceptible everywhere, and being somewhat cloudy the usual glare of a closing hot summer day was dispelled, thus further aiding the solemn appearance as I approached the sacred acres. To my surprise I found two cemeteries instead of one, for nestling close to the larger (the Government) I discovered

THE HEBREWS' REST,

the place of interment of the ancient, industrious and irrepressible race who trace their genealogy to the patriarchs who wandered with Moses, sung and fought with David, imbibed the wisdom of Solomon and in our own age produced such intellectual giants as Britain's Beaconsfield and Leon Gambetta, the genius of the successful Republic of France. A few feet more and I was at the

SACRED CAMP-GROUND,

where lie interred, according to the record in the office, three thousand two hundred and seventy-four soldiers and sailors who, during our late fratricidal struggle, wore the blue. They are from nearly every State that belonged to the Federal constellation of stars.

The grounds are well enclosed with a handsome and substantial brick wall, and near the first gate stands the keeper's lodge, a neat little cottage, which in architecture is a remarkably fine adaptation (considering its small size) of the French chateau style. It is built of that wonderful composite, shells petrified and imbedded in clay, which Nature has been perfecting for centuries in her mighty laboratories near New Bern, and which for cemetery enclosures or buildings, on account of its venerable appearance, seems to be even better adapted than the most flawless Parian marble. It is crowned by a slated mansard in perfect harmony with the building and surroundings; English ivy fondly clings to its side, and the air is perfumed with the sweetest and choicest of flowers. A model stable stands in the rear, built of material similar to the lodge. This combination, backed by the forest of trees, the varying tints of tombstones, shrubbery, grass and deep-hued flowers, makes, particularly when the golden sun is setting, an enchanting picture, which at once fascinates the eye and charms the heart.

The grounds are grand and rank among the best efforts of landscape gardening in the State. It is true there is the usual monotony which will always acompany Government cemeteries as long as the regulation headstones are used, but there is a wealth of rich, velvety lawns and such a great variety of stately trees, so well placed that they make up to a great extent for the tiresome effect produced by these War Department slabs. In the centre a tall flag-pole protrudes from a well-designed iron base, ornamented with wreaths, torches, eagles, leaves, etc. To the left and near the road is

SYLVAN HALL,

a happy combination of maple-trees so arranged as to form a large space, which assumes shape in the form of a Latin cross. In the centre, one can easily believe himself as being within the walls of some stately cathedral and realize how the Gothic style of architecture originated.

Darkness had already thrown her black cloak over the earth and shut out New Bern from my sight, when I bid the guardian of the dead good-night and left him at his melancholy post of duty, left him to his lonesome calling and solemn surroundings, turned my horse towards living New Bern and soon found myself on the road, with the broad, rippling, ever-moving, but tireless, Neuse to my left, and in half an hour I once again stood in the hospitable-looking office of the Hotel Albert, its cheerful surroundings a remarkable contrast to the place I had just left—New Bern's camp-ground of the Federal war quota to that great and ever-increasing army that defies no enemy and holds no malice.

NEW BERN'S BUSINESS AND BUSINESS MEN.

Population, 7,500; leading interests, cotton, rice, fish, trucking, naval stores, oysters, game, mercantile and manufacturing; railroad, Atlantic & North Carolina, Washington Bryan, President, S. L. Dill, Superintendent; steam-boat lines, Old Dominion Steam-ship Company, Capt. E. B. Roberts, Agent; Neuse and Trent River Steam-boat Company, J. M. White, General Manager, J. J. Dissosway, Agent; Eastern Carolina Dispatch, Geo. Henderson, Agent; N. C. Freight Line, S. H. Gray, Agent; Hyde Line, W. P. Burrus, Manager.

The following list embraces New Bern's most energetic and enterprising business establishments on January 1st, 1888:

Agricultural Implements and Hardware.
George Allen & Co.
J. C. Whitty, Craven street.

Architect and Builder.
C. J. Scheelky.

Banks.
National, John Hughes, President; Geo. Allen, Vice-President.
Green, Foy & Co.

Boots and Shoes.
W. E. Patterson (under Hotel Albert).

Commission Merchants, Brokers, and Dealers in Meat.
E. K. Bishop.
W. F. Rountree.

Clothiers.
George Ash, Middle street.
Max Schuvern.

Drugs, Patent Medicines, Perfumes, &c.

F. S. Duffy, Middle street.
Hancock Bros.
R. N. Duffy, N. W. cor. Pollock and Middle streets.
J. V. Jordon, N. W. cor. Broad and Middle streets.
Leinster Duffy, West End.

Dry Goods (Wholesale and Retail).

O. A. Marks, Pollock street.
A. M. Baker.

Dry Goods and Clothing.

M. H. Sultan.
J. S. Cohen, Middle street.
M. Cohen, Middle street.
F. T. Patterson, Middle street.
J. F. Ives, Middle street.
Wm. Sultan, Middle street.
H. B. Duffy, Middle street.

Furniture, Mattresses, &c.

John Suter, Middle street.
New Bern Furniture Store, J. M. Hines, Manager.

General Merchandise.

B. B. Davenport, foot Middle street.
Jas. F. Taylor, next to Last Chance, Middle street.
S. H. Lane, Agent (Ship Chandler).
J. J. Wolfenden.

Groceries.

Alex. Justice (wholesale and retail).
Dail Bros. (wholesale and retail).
Wm. Colligan, at Depot.

Hardware (General).

Smallwood & Slover.
L. H. Cutler, Middle street.

Insurance and Real Estate Agents.
W. B. Boyd (Notary Public).
W. G. Brinson.

Insurance—Life, Fire, Marine and Accidental.
W. H. Oliver.
Watson & Street.

Jewelry, Diamonds and Watches.
Bell, Middle street.
Sam. K. Eaton, Middle street.

Liquors, Wines, &c. (Wholesale).
James Redmond. (See advertisement).

Livery, Sale and Exchange Stables.
M. Hahn & Co., Middle street.
J. W. Stewart, Broad street, between Middle and Hancock.

Manufactories.
Thos. S. Howard, Steam Marine Railway and Shipyard.
T. F. Hall & Bro., Gunsmiths and Hotel Electric Bells.
C. T. Randolph, Carriage and general repairing.
John H. Crabtree & Co., Machinists, Founders and Blacksmiths.
Willis & Edwards, Machinists, Founders and Blacksmiths.
E. M. Pavie, Carpenter and Builder.
J. A. Simpson, Contractor, Builder and Undertaker.
Joe K. Willis, Cemetery and Building work of all kinds.
C. Erdman, Cigar Factory.

Photographer.
Edward Gerock, Middle street.

Pianos and Organs.

Adolph Cohen, cor. Broad and Middle streets.

Taxidermy.

Miss A. W. Duffy.

Undertaker.

George Bishop.

Agricultural (Shell) Lime.

W. P. Burrus & Co., Market Dock.

Commission (Cotton and Rice).

S. W. & E. W. Smallwood.

Confectioner (Wholesale and Retail).

John Dunn.

Crockery, Glass and Willow-ware.

Alex. Miller, 61 and 63 Broad street.

Gentlemen's Furnishing Goods.

Howard & Jones.

Sausage, Pork and Fresh Meats.

Charles E. Nelson, Broad street.

School Books and Stationery.

Henry L. Hall, Middle street.

KINSTON, N. C.

Well situated upon the banks of the Neuse, which to this point is navigable for steam-boats all the year round, stands the city of Kinston.

Its streets are broad and regularly laid out. Queen, its main business thoroughfare, gives a splendid opportunity for this little city to display her business buildings, the majority of which are substantial structures, well designed and built mostly of brick, with iron columns, caps, cornices and other ornaments.

The streets upon which the residences are located are also broad and well shaded by two lines of trees, with the exception of King street, which not only has its sidewalks protected from the sun's rays by well-cared-for, wide-spreading elms, but also casts a grateful shade over travelers in vehicles and their weary beasts through the agency of another line through the centre.

The residences, generally speaking, are neat, with large front yards in which flowers and shrubbery show that the inhabitants have an appreciation for nature as well as architecture.

The churches of Kinston are well adapted for the uses of the various congregations that own them, are well attended, have a neat, cheerful appearance, and some have excellent accoustic properties, but as they are all built of perishable material (wood), it is not within the province of this book to give them a special description.

Having described the general features of this pretty little city, it is now necessary to point out its special attractions, foremost among which is

LENOIR COUNTY COURT-HOUSE,

a most imposing structure, well situated in the very heart of this, one of the North State's loveliest county-seats.

Its massive square Norman tower and great clock give it (for the Carolinas) an unusual appearance, but adds much to the beauty of the town, not only when its entire well-proportioned elevations are visible, but also when at a distance it is observed as a break in the sky-line, towering high over the many roofs and green trees of Kinston.

The next most prominent erection is

THE CASWELL MONUMENT,

which stands in the centre of the crossing of Queen and Caswell streets, and is one of the few public memorials in North Carolina that is not secreted in a cemetery. It is built of enduring granite and stands upon a small mound created for the purpose. It was erected to perpetuate the memory of

RICHARD CASWELL,

who, without a doubt, was one of the grandest types of pure manhood of the Colonial, Revolutionary and early National period. Born in Maryland, he left that colony early in life with a surveyor's compass on his shoulder and settled in North Carolina. He soon became so thoroughly identified with his new surroundings that he gained the esteem and confidence of both the people and government, who delighted in honoring him and placing him in positions of trust. When, in 1771, Tryon made his march against the Regulators, Colonel Caswell was Speaker of the Colonial Assembly, and followed him to the banks of the Alamance. He loyally clung to the Crown until Britain's laws, King and Governors became unbearable, when he joined his adopted colony and united country in the successful revolution which placed the newborn Republic among the greatest of nations.

This distinguished statesman and soldier, besides holding nearly every other position of trust within the gift of North Carolina, both in State and Colony, was four times her Governor.

The Opera House is a well-designed brick building, which adds much to the good appearance of Queen street, but the

HOTEL TULL

is the most imposing structure in the city, and, with the exception of the court-house, is the costliest and most impressive in the county. It is built of brick, three stories in height, including its well-proportioned mansard roof, pierced by many deeply-recessed windows.

I know of no better way of concluding this hasty sketch than by a few words upon

RIVERSIDE PARK,

or, as it should be called, Parrott Park, in honor of Mr. J. F. Parrott, who owns the land, but generously ceded it for a number of years to the citizens of Kinston to be used as a public pleasure. It is on the opposite shore of the Neuse and is approached by a bridge across the river, which overlooks the busy landing of the Neuse and Trent Navigation Company, and when these steamers and barges are being loaded the active scene adds much to the general effect.

Upon entering the park one is much impressed with the diversity of its natural features; it looks as if Nature made her best endeavor to perfect it. The rolling ground, well covered with choice grasses, perennial bushes and clumps of great trees, forms many handsome landscape effects. The citizens of Kinston take great interest in this lovely resort and have shown considerable taste and skill in its improvement. Brush and trees have been removed where they obstructed a view and others have been added when they would ensure a charming vista. Flowers have been planted to assist their wild companions in perfuming the atmosphere and pleasing the eye with their many-tinted hues. Rustic seats have been placed in many shaded spots and paths cut in many directions, so lovers have their choice, on a summer's eve, when planning their future, to either sit and chat in secluded arbors or to meander by the river side with flashing fireflies for their companions and the whispering Neuse a fit accompaniment to their words of love.

KINSTON AS A BUSINESS POINT.

Population, 2,700; leading business interests, cotton, mercantile and manufacturing; railroad, Atlantic & North Carolina; steam-boat line, Neuse and Trent Steam-boat Company, J. M. White, General Manager.

The following is a list of Kinston's leading business houses on January 1st, 1888:

Bakers and Confectioners.

McRae & Bizzell, Queen street.

Dentist.
H. D. Harper, D. D. S., office in Opera House.

Drugs, Patent Medicines, Perfumery, &c.
R. F. Whitehurst, Queen street.
Henry Dunn, Queen street.
John E. Parrott, Queen street.

General Merchandise.
S. H. Abbott, Queen street.

Dry Goods, Clothing, Boots and Shoes.
C. W. Burt, Queen street.

Hardware, Stoves, Building Material.
B. W. Carady, Queen street.

Jewelry, Watches and Clocks.
C. Bailey, Queen street.

Manufacturers.
E. M. Hodges, Wagons and Carts.
Geo. B. Webb, Carriage-maker and Undertaker.
J. C. Hay, Cabinet-maker and Undertaker.
S. H. Abbott, Bricks and Tiles.

Machinery, Engines, Buggies and Wagons.
J. W. Granger, Queen street.

Navigation Company.
Neuse and Trent River, J. M. White, Manager.

Restaurant.
"May's," J. D. May, Proprietor.

Real Estate and General Auctioneer.
C. W. Burt, Queen street.

BAYBORO AND STONEWALL,

THE TWINS OF PAMLICO.

Bayboro and Stonewall, the rival villages of Pamlico county, are pleasantly situated, the first at, the other near, the head of navigation of Bay river.

The villages are separated by about one mile and a quarter of woodland, river, marsh and cultivated fields. The rivalry between these two little towns makes itself manifest at the church fairs which always take place in one or the other twice a year during the sessions of the Superior Court of Pamlico County. It is the custom at these fairs to ascertain by vote which of the towns contains the prettiest girl, and one is selected from each as a fit subject for the suffrage of citizens and strangers. The voters do not have to register, and all the qualification they require is twenty-five cents for each ballot cast. Repeating is allowed until the money gives out, and many a young man who has indulged in this pleasantry has had to economize for weeks after to get even. After the votes are counted the successful candidate receives a handsome shawl, which is always presented by the leader of the opposing faction.

Both towns are well situated, and with the inevitable growth of the back country, which must use them as shipping and trading points, they are destined to grow towards each other until they become one city.

The facilities for water transportation are good for steam-boats and small sailing craft.

Each of the towns contains about two hundred inhabitants, enjoys a fair retail trade, manufactures considerable lumber and some flour, but as yet have no buildings which require a special description.

The following is a list of the leading business houses of Bayboro on January 1st, 1888:

Drugs, Patent Medicines, Perfumery, &c.
" Pioneer," Cowell & Gates, Proprietors.

General Merchandise.
Fowler & Cowell.
J. B. Turner.
W. H. Sawyer & Co.

Manufacturers.
Miller & Hooker, Lumber.
Fowler & Cowell, Steam Grist, Flour and Corn Mills.

The following is a list of the leading business houses of Stonewall on January 1st, 1888:

General Merchandise.
C. H. Fowler.
J. B. Ferebee.
S. W. Ferebee.

Groceries and Confectioneries.
S. J. Lane.

Manufactories.
Bay River Lumber Company and Pamlico Steam Saw-mills, A. H. Whitcomb, Manager.
Fowler's Grist-mill.

AURORA, N. C.

Auroro, at the head of navigation of South river, is well situated in the very centre of the celebrated "richlands" of Beaufort county. These lands are generally conceded as being among the most productive, in an agricultural point of view, in the State, the product being mainly cotton, corn, rice and potatoes. Two bales of cotton, one hundred and ten bushels of corn, sixty-five bushels of rice and three hundrd bushels of sweet potatoes have each been raised to the acre on the virgin soil without the use of any of the farmer's bankrupting material (imported fertilizers).

This little city is well laid out and bids fair to become a still greater trade centre. It is blessed with an academy which has made excellent reputation, and has an active, pushing business population.

The following is a list of the leading business houses of Auroro on January 1st, 1888:

Educational.

Auroro Academy (male and female), R. T. Bonner, Principal.

Banking, Dry Goods, Groceries. &c.

J. B. Bonner.

Drugs, Patent Medicines, Perfumery, &c.

G. D. Langston.

General Merchandise.

F. F. Cherry (Watches and Jewelry).
W. H. Gaskins.
J. B. Crawford.
J. B. Bryan & Son.

Feed, Sale and Exchange Stables.

Wm. Harvey.

WASHINGTON, N. C.,

NORTH CAROLINA'S SHIP-YARD.

NOTE.—This description of Washington, like that of Edenton, with the exception of the article on the parks, I wrote for, and was published in, the *News and Observer* of Raleigh, in the year which has just come to an end, and as the intervening space of time has been too short to allow any great change, I am satisfied it is a faithful picture of Washington as it is when this book leaves the press.

On the north bank of the Pamlico river, just thirty-five miles from where it loses its identity by mingling its waters with those of the sound bearing the same name, is situated a little city containing about 4,000 inhabitants, which to-day exhibits the busiest water-front, with one exception (Wilmington), in the State of North Carolina. She is the fortunate possessor of a number of well-constructed, cleanly-kept wharves, to which are tied in great numbers every conceivable craft that registers 500 or less tons, in fact, any vessel that can come over Hatteras bar, which means anything below a square-rigger (ship or bark), can tie up at the wharves of Washington, N. C., and besides the hum, the din and the refreshing activity of an active port, the eye is gratified by the vision, on a small scale, of that—to America— almost lost art, ship-building, for at the time of my visit on the stocks of one of its three ship-yards (Capt. Styron's) the largest steamer ever built in North Carolina was under construction. She was to be of four hundred tons burthen and to be owned by a local transportation company.

This little city owns six large sea-going vessels, engaged in the West India trade, eight steamers and a large fleet of smaller craft. These facts, coupled with the following, I am satisfied will convince the reader that its future is indeed assured, for the steamers of five transportation lines dot every navigable sound and stream on their way to or from this active mart; one line of railroad connects it at Jamesville with the Roanoke river, and a new line is projected, which will take her out of her former seclusion and connect her with the railroad system of the entire nation. Her

PUBLIC BUILDINGS

are just three in number, and all are situated on Market street; the court-house at one end, the town hall at the other end; sandwiched in between the two, with a small vacant lot between each, is the combined county and city jail. This is exceedingly convenient, as courts are held in both the municipal and county buildings and the jail can be kept full by having prisoners "fired" in from two different directions.

The court-house is a well-constructed two-and-a-half-story brick building, ornamented at one end with a high tower, in which is placed the clock which apprises the good citizens that time never tires, unless the clock gets out of repair. At the other end prominently hangs the worst sounding bell that ever summoned a juror or embarrassed a witness. Its horrible tintinnabulation is sufficient to throw into convulsions judges made of less stern stuff than those that grace North Carolina's Bench.

I wrote these lines in the hotel office and read them to the judge, two resident attorneys and a number of other citizens that were seated around the stove and informed them that if in their judgment they would give offense, I would not send them in for publication, but all of them earnestly, and some, I think, "tearfully implored" me to have them printed, with the hope that it will cause it to be replaced by one that will not prove a terror to any unfortunates living within the sound of its harsh and grating tone. The jail is a solid two-story building, the monotony of its red brick front relieved by the regulation iron bars.

But the pride of the town, in an architectural point of view, is

THE TOWN HALL,

built in 1884; it has an impressive brick and stone front, with large ornamental arch windows filled with stained glass, and is capped by a Venetian dome. The upper floor is a handsomely decorated and nicely furnished hall, and the lower contains the city's fire apparatus, which consists of three powerful engines of *ante-bellum* pattern and a fully equipped hook and ladder truck.

Washington was at the very height of her prosperity when the conflict between the States commenced. This is well attested by two substantial bank buildings, which show considerable architectural pretensions in the way of Doric and Ionic columns. One of these buildings is used for a drug store, the other for a law office and dwelling. With

CHURCHES

the town is well supplied. The Episcopal is a large brick building, mantled with ivy. Its interior is impressively decorated, and a number of large windows, through the agency of cathedral-stained glass, admit the much-sought-for, dim, religious light. It is surrounded by a large, well-kept church-yard, in which, under many beautiful monuments, are buried that part of Washington's population which died in the Episcopal faith.

The Presbyterian church is built of the same material, but in an entirely different style. It is a solid-looking structure and is also surrounded by a well-cared-for grave-yard. The Methodist church is also of brick, and also surrounded by a little church-yard, ornamented with costly monuments and refreshing shrubbery. While standing in front of this church taking mental notes for this article, an incident occurred which will not soon fade from my mind. I was approached by a pleasant-looking lady, her face beaming with a pure religious smile. She informed me that Sunday-school was about to commence and that strangers had a standing invitation to attend. I am hardly rated as much of a religious man, but I could not help but calculate the amount of good that would be done if other ladies would follow the religious example of the pastor's good wife of Washington, and came to the conclusion that with many of the great army that find it necessary to travel on business, or have the wealth to see the world on pleasure tours, novels would give way to the Bible, and chess and checkers to Prayer-books, on Sunday.

All cities, large and small, have some peculiar or prominent features that distinguish them from others, and Washington is no exception. What would attract the attention of the observing stranger most is of a nature almost too grave to speak about. It is the great number of

GRAVE-YARDS

situated within the corporate limits. Besides the three already described four more exist, and three of these have their main front on the second most important business thoroughfare in the city (Market street). From this it would appear to the superficial observer that Washington is a good place to die as well as to live in, but if he will enquire he will find that the health here is as good as that of any other town of its size in the country. The cause of so many small cemeteries is that North Carolina Washingtonians believe in burying their dead around the respective churches, and there certainly seems to be no more appropriate location for God's-acre than that surrounding the house in which He is worshiped. Washington also contains

A MARINE PARK,

pleasantly situated upon Main street. Under the shade of some of its wide-spreading mulberry trees quietly repose some monster, formidable-looking masses of iron, which, although neatly painted and picturesquely placed, look so grim and forbidding that they are liable to deceive a stranger into the belief that they are intended to hurl missiles of destruction in time of war, but that is a mistake, for a closer inspection will show that instead of monsters for destruction they are designed to be warning angels, and to show confused mariners where danger in form of sunken shoals and treacherous reefs exists.

She also has an opportuity of constructing still another park at little expense, which would unquestionably be the most striking and pleasing in the State, for opposite the town is a pretty little island well adapted by nature for park purposes. At the present time its natural beauties are disfigured by a number of wretched looking sheds, and the aroma from the foliage that shades it gives way to the effluvia eminating from the guano stored within their frail sides.

But what will make Washington most prominent and give her reputation far and wide is her

CONFEDERATE MONUMENT,

which is to be erected in a very short time, not in an obscure cemetery where few strangers will see it or upon even the most prominent square, where all who visit that locality can only glance at it, but at the down-stream limit of the city, on the very highest point washed by the murmuring waters of the superb Pamlico, upon the top of a former Federal fort made to guard the city and prevent the entrance of the very men whose deeds are to be perpetuated, upon a pedestal of enduring granite, will stand, gun in hand, the statue of a soldier of the Confederacy.

The mariner, as he sails in from Pamlico Sound, will see this sentinel twelve miles away, and from the base of the statue the eye of the spectator beholds a view that is seldom equalled: to the west, the active, well-shaded city, with a water-front well lined with shipping; north, the many tints peculiar to a North Carolina forest; south, the broad Pamlico, and east, the same stream, as far as the eye can reach, as with a number of graceful curves it rolls on to the sound, seemingly murmuring a requiem to the Confederate dead.

THE BUSINESS AND BUSINESS MEN OF WASHINGTON.

Population, 3,500; leading interests, manufacturing, ship-building, shipping, fishing, cotton and mercantile.

The following is a list of the leading houses of Washington on January 1st, 1888:

Banker.

C. M. Brown.

Commission Merchants.

John Myers & Son.
J. R. B. Havens (Miller).
J. M. Gaskill.

Confectioneries, Toys and Fancy Goods.
C. H. Sterling.
Dentist.
Dr. H. Snell, Main street. (Gas administered).
Drugs, Patent Medicines, Perfumery, &c.
D. N. Bogart (under Opera House).
Dr. D. T. Tayloe.
Dr. S. T. Nicholson & Bro.

Dry Goods and Clothing.
A. W. Thomas.
D. T. Swindell.
H. Morris & Bros.

Furniture.
J. A. Burgess.

General Merchandise.
W. B. Morton & Co.
S. Spencer Bros., cor. Market and Main streets.
M. T. Archbell, Main street.
J. F. Buckman.
C. W. Tayloe (Cotton Buyer).

Groceries (Wholesale).
S. R. Fowle & Son.

Groceries (Wholesale and Retail).
John B. Sparrow.
E. K. Willis, Water street, east of Market.
B. W. Bergerson, East Market Square.
D. R. Willis, East Market Square.

Hardware, Stoves and Tinware.
W. C. Mallison.

Harness, Saddles, Whips, &c.
T. E. Warren.

Insurance.

R. C. Montgomery, General Agent (Life and Fire).
Mutual Live Stock Company.

Jewelers.

John Bell, Jr.
J. C. Morton.

Livery, Sale, Feed and Exchange Stables.

S. H. Bailey.
J. G. Chauncy.

Machinery (General Agent).

O. K. Stilley.

Marble Monuments, Fertilizers and Baled Cotton.

W. J. Crumpler.

Marine Railway.

"Pamlico," J. Myers & Son, Proprietors.

Manufacturers.

Myers' Cotton Seed Oil Mills, Jno. Myers, Proprietor.
E. M. Short, Lumber.
W. N. Archbell, Lumber.
Geo. W. Kugler & Son, Lumber.
B. F. Rodman, Iron Works and Foundry.
C. W. Phillips, Carriage Factory.
Ed. Long, Carriages, Buggies, &c.
D. S. Lidden, Ship-builder and Contractor.

Tobacco, Snuff and Cigars (Wholesale and Retail).

S. H. Williams.

Towing Company.

Pickles Bros., Proprietors; W. Pickles, General Manager.

THE PRESS

OF NORFOLK, PORTSMOUTH AND SOME OF THE PRINCIPAL CITIES OF NORTH CAROLINA.

What the four cardinal points are to the compass the Press, the Church, the Schools and the Law are to the community, and nowhere does the first, the acknowledged champion of right and the greatest opposing force to wrong, exert a greater influence than in Norfolk, Portsmouth and the Sound and River Cities of North Carolina. In tone, it is moral. There is no paper published in this section that would permit a line to disfigure its columns which would cause a blush to mantle, the brow of the most refined lady, or that is unfit to be read by children. Generally speaking, they can be classed conservative, except during the heat of a political campaign, when they are very decided, and throw their entire weight and energy with the party whose cause they espouse.

For the benefit of advertisers and other interested parties, I concluded to make a special Press list instead of arranging the following well-known and acknowledged champions, educators and mouth-pieces of the people at the conclusion of the description of their respective cities.

NORFOLK, VA.

Virginian, daily; *Virginian and Carolinian*, weekly; Henry E. Orr, Editor; M. Glennan, Proprietor. Address, "Virginian."

Landmark, daily and weekly; S. S. Nottingham, Jr., Editor. Address, "Landmark Publishing Co."

Public Ledger, evening; Edwards & Fiveash, Editors and Proprietors. Address, "Public Ledger."

Telegram, daily; Christian Voice Publishing Company, Publishers. Address, R. E. Turner, Manager.

Christian Voice, semi-weekly; R. E. Turner, Editor; Christian Voice Publishing Company, Proprietors.

Norfolk Progress, weekly; R. F. Woodward, Editor; Progress Publishing Company, Proprietors.

Journal of Commerce, weekly; W. Tompson Barron, Editor and Proprietor.

Herald, weekly; W. S. Copes, Editor and Proprietor.

Cornucopia, monthly; A Jeffers, Editor. Address, "Cornucopia."

PORTSMOUTH, VA.

Enterprise, daily; J. W. H. Porter, Editor and Proprietor.

Times, daily and weekly; J. H. Wilcox, Editor and Proprietor.

CHAPEL HILL, N. C.

University Monthly, Literary Societies of North Carolina University, Editors and Proprietors.

DURHAM, N. C.

Recorder, daily and weekly; E. C. Hackney, Editor and Proprietor.

Tobacco Plant, weekly; W. G. Burkhead, Editor.

EDENTON, N. C.

Fisherman and Farmer, semi-weekly; A. H. Mitchell, Editor and Manager.

ELIZABETH CITY, N. C.

Economist, weekly; R. B. Creecy, Editor and Proprietor.

Falcon, weekly; Falcon Publishing Company, Proprietors.
North Carolinian, weekly; Palemon John, Editor and Proprietor.

FAYETTEVILLE, N. C.

Observer, weekly; Geo. H. Haigh, Editor and Proprietor.
News, weekly; J. H. Benton and W. M. Dicker, Editors and Proprietors.

GOLDSBORO, N. C.

Argus, daily and weekly; J. E. Robinson, Editor and Proprietor.

GREENVILLE, N. C.

Eastern Reflector, weekly; J. R. Wichard, Editor and Proprietor.
Democratic Standard, G. B. King, Editor and Proprietor.

HENDERSON, N. C.

Henderson News, weekly; A. Hatchett, Editor.
Gold Leaf, weekly; Thad. R. Manning, Editor and Proprietor.

HILLSBORO, N. C.

Orange County Observer, weekly; Joseph A. Harris, Editor and Proprietor.
Recorder, weekly; Parrish & Strudwick, Editors and Proprietors.

KINSTON, N. C.

Free Press, weekly.

LA GRANGE, N. C.

Davis Cadet, monthly; Davis & Co., Proprietors.

LOUISBURG, N. C.

Franklin Times, weekly; J. A. Thomas, Editor and Proprietor.

MURFREESBORO, N. C.

Index, weekly; J. W. Hicks, Editor and Proprietor.

NEW BERN, N. C.

Journal, daily and weekly; H. S. Nunn, Editor; Nunn & Harper, Proprietors.
Free-Will Baptist, weekly; R. K. Hearn, Editor.

OXFORD, N. C.

Orphan's Friend, weekly; L. Thomas, Manager.
Torchlight, weekly; E. W. Jones & Co., Editors and Proprietors.

PITTSBORO, N. C.

Chatham Record, weekly; H. A. London, Editor and Proprietor.
Home, weekly; A. H. Merritt, Editor and Proprietor.

PLYMOUTH, N. C.

Sun, E. L. Foster, Editor and Proprietor.

RALEIGH, N. C.

News and Observer, daily and weekly; J. I. McRee, Editor. Address, "News and Observer Publishing Company."
Evening Visitor, daily; Brown & Utley, Editors and Proprietors.
State Chronicle, weekly; Josephus Daniels, Editor; Chronicle Publishing Company, Proprietors.

Biblical Recorder, weekly (Baptist); Rev. C. T. Bailey, Editor and Proprietor.
Christian Advocate, weekly (Methodist); Rev. F. L. Reid, Editor and Proprietor.
Christian Sun, weekly (Christian); Rev. J. P. Barrett, Editor and Proprietor.
Signal, weekly; J. C. L. Harris, Editor.
The North Carolina Teacher, E. G. Harrell, Editor.
North Carolina Farmer, monthly; James H. Enniss, Editor and Proprietor.
Progressive Farmer, weekly; L. L. Polk, Editor.
Spirit of the Age (devoted to temperance); Rev. R. H. Whitaker, Editor and Proprietor.

SMITHFIELD, N. C.

Herald, weekly; F. T. Booker, Editor and Proprietor.

SOUTHERN PINES, N. C.

Pine Knot, weekly; B. A. Goodridge, Editor and Proprietor.

TARBORO, N. C.

Southerner, weekly; F. Powell, Editor and Proprietor.

WAKE FOREST, N. C.

Wake Forest Student, monthly; Literary Societies of Wake Forest College, Editors and Proprietors.

WASHINGTON, N. C.

Gazette, weekly; H. A. Latham, Editor and Proprietor.
Progress, weekly; Dr. A. B. Chapin, Editor.

WILMINGTON, N. C.

Messenger, daily and weekly; J. A. Bonitz, Editor; Messenger Publishing Company, Proprietors.
Star, daily and weekly; T. B. Kingsbury, Editor; W. H. Bernard, Proprietor.
Review, daily and weekly; Josh T. James, Editor and Proprietor.
North Carolina Presbyterian, weekly; John McLaurin, Editor and Proprietor.
North Carolina Medical Journal, monthly; Thomas S. Wood, M. D., Editor.

WINDSOR, N. C.

Ledger, weekly; W. H. Swain, Editor and Proprietor.

WINTON, N. C.

Monitor, weekly; P. H. Welch, Editor and Proprietor.

ATTORNEYS

OF NORFOLK AND PART OF NORTH CAROLINA.

This profession, which requires more individual force, strength of character, tireless energy and inborn talent, as well as educated brain, than any other, is well represented in Norfolk and North Carolina by gentlemen " whose skill as advocates," whose reputation in defending clients and whose honorable transactions and foremost standing in their respective social circles are well known throughout the land. Although they are outnumbered by nearly every other calling, they have produced more statesmen and have been called upon to represent the people in the councils of both Nation and State more than all the others combined.

These brilliant gentlemen, many of whose voices have echoed through the legislative halls of Washington, Richmond and Raleigh, are retained by many leading firms, both North and South, to attend to their collecting, as well as other legal business, and for the convenience of my patrons who may require counsel I have arranged their names and addresses in one continuous list.

The reason that the Norfolk Bar is not better represented is strictly my own fault, as I delayed seeing its members until near the completion of the book, when the great quantity of work to be done in a limited time prevented my seeing them.

NORFOLK, VA.

Starke & Martin, 74 and 76 Main street.
Walke & Old, 72 Main street, Lowenburg Building.
Whitehurst & Hughes, 78 Main street, Lowenburg Building.
H. L. Worthington, 125 Main street.
Bruce Simmons, 78 Main street.

AURORA, N. C.

Thomas W. Mayhew.

BAYBORO, N. C.

W. T. Caho.

COLUMBIA, N. C.

R. P. Felton. Edmund Alexander.

DURHAM, N. C.

W. W. Fuller.
E. C. Hackney.
John S. Moring.

Manning & Manning.
J. A. Long.
Strudwick & Boone.

EDENTON, N. C.

Pruden & Vann.
Julian Wood.

Wm. W. Bond.
Samuel J. Skinner.

ELIZABETH CITY, N. C.

Lamb & Riddle.
J. W. Albertson & Son.
Frank Vaughan.

Grandy & Aydlett.
J. Heywood Sawyer.
Griffin & Temple.

FRANKLINTON, N. C.

B. F. Bullock.

GREENVILLE, N. C.

Isaac A. Sugg.

Latham, Skinner & Blow.

GOLDSBORO, N. C.

Nixon & Galloway.

GATESVILLE, N. C.

St. Leon Scull.

L. L. Smith.

HERTFORD, N. C.

T. G. Skinner.

W. N. Newbold.
Blount & Blount.

HENDERSON, N. C.

Walter R. Henry.

A. C. Zollicoffer.

KINSTON, N. C.

J. F. Wooten.
O. H. Allen.
Ashley T. Hill.
N. J. Rouse.

M. A. Gray.
A. J. Loftin & G. Rountree.
Jackson & Perry.
C. H. Brown.

LOUISBURG, N. C.

C. M. Cooke.

MURFREESBORO, N. C.

Winborne & Bro.

MANTEO, N. C.

J. M. Gray.

NEW BERN, N. C.

Simmons & Manly.
Clarke & Clarke.
M. D. W. Stevenson.
Leonidas J. Moore.

L. J. Moore.
Wm. E. Clarke.
George Green.
Henry R. Bryan.

O. H. Guion.

OXFORD, N. C.

L. C. Edwards. Graham & Winston.
J. M. Sikes.

PLYMOUTH, N. C.

Latham & Pettigrew. S. B. Spruill, Jr.

RALEIGH, N. C.

John W. Hinsdale.
John Gatling.
Fuller & Snow.

Haywood & Haywood.
Reade, Busbee & Busbee.
Strong, Gray & Stamps.

Peele & Maynard. Argo & Fleming.
Armistead Jones. Spier Whitaker.
T. R. Purnell. Oct. Coke.
J. C. L. Harris. Devereux & Wilder.
Batchelor & Devereux.

ROCKY MOUNT, N. C.

B. H. Bunn.

SHAWBORO, N. C.

W. B. Shaw.

TARBORO, N. C.

H. A. Gilliam & Son.

WASHINGTON, N. C.

W. B. Rodman & Son. John H. Small.
E. S. Simmons. Charles U. Hill.
George I. Sparrow. George H. Brown, Jr.

WINDSOR, N. C.

J. B. Martin. Winston & Williams.
Duncan C. Winston.

WINTON, N. C.

George Cowper. P. B. Picot.

WARRENTON, N. C.

C. A. Cooke. W. A. Montgomery.
W. H. Polk.

WELDON, N. C.

Day & Zollicoffer.

THE FISHING INTEREST.

THE FISHERMEN AND FISH SHIPPERS OF THE SOUND AND RIVER DISTRICT OF NORTH CAROLINA.

If the reader will take a map of North Carolina and then arm himself with a lead-pencil, put the point of it where the Virginia boundary intersects the 77th degree of west longitude, run a line down this meridian to 34° 30' north latitude, and then allow the pencil to make an ocean trip on that parallel to 75° 30' west longitude, and run up that meridian to opposite the boundary line alluded to above, and on that dividing line to the starting point, he will enclose one of the grandest and most profitable fishing sections on the face of the globe.

Within these lines, which embrace a land and water area about one-fifth the size of the State of North Carolina, is situated the whole of Albemarle Sound, with the best part of its great tributaries, the Chowan and the Roanoke, as well as lesser streams, like the Alligator, Scuppernong, Pasquotank, Perquimans, etc., all teeming with the choicest varieties of fish. Here is also the whole of great Pamlico Sound, with its wonderful oyster beds, and the mouths of the mighty Neuse and broad Pamlico, the whole of Currituck and several smaller sounds.

In this district over five thousand fishermen find employment in taking from their natural element the great staple of the sound and river district of North Carolina—fish, which include the standard herring, the toothsome shad, the highly prized rock, the monster sturgeon, besides white perch, trout, hickory-shad, blue-fish, mullets, mackerel, menhaden, speckled perch, bass, pike, flounders, eels, cat-fish and the latest addition to profitable fishing, the comical-looking porpoise. The list can be swelled with the many varieties of shell-fish that are annually taken and shipped to Northern markets as well as consumed at home.

The following is a list of many of the leading shippers and proprietors of fisheries:

COLUMBIA, TYRRELL COUNTY, N. C.

James A. Halloway.
J. A. Rhodes.
Joseph W. Spruill.
W. H. H. Cooper.
F. R. Rhodes.
H. W. Hayman.
Woodley & Spruill.
John D. Snell.
Gilbert Bateman.
A. B. Snell.
T. L. Jones.

COLERAINE, BERTIE COUNTY, N. C.

Wilson & Mizell.

CURRITUCK COURT HOUSE, N. C.

W. H. Bray.
B. Ballance.
S. B. Hughes.
A. W. Brumsey.
G. A. Tatum.
Dennis Brabble.
A. W. Parker.
W. Ballance.
Caleb Ballance.
Luke Pool.
E. M. Walker.

COINJOCK, CURRITUCK COUNTY, N. C.

B. F. Barco.
J. B. Jarvis.
W. J. Walker.
S. D. Walker.
S. Ballance.
Henry Welsted.
Charles Forbes.

EDENTON, N. C.

W. D. Rea.
John C. Bond.

Shepard, Goodwin & Co.
W. L. Arendell & Co.

ELIZABETH CITY, N. C.

Capt. Sam. Waters.

GOOSE CREEK ISLAND, PAMLICO COUNTY, N. C.

D. B. Sadler.

HERTFORD, PERQUIMANS COUNTY, N. C.

J. J. Parrish.

KITTY HAWK, CURRITUCK COUNTY, N. C.

J. P. Pugh.

LAKE LANDING, HYDE COUNTY, N. C.

T. P. Pugh.

MANTEO, DARE COUNTY, N. C.

A. J Miller.
John Q. Homer.
George C. Daniels.

L. M. Midgett.
E. Meekins, Jr.
S. E. Mann.

MANN'S HARBOR, DARE COUNTY N. C.

William Mann.
Avery Tillet.
Edward Mann.
James T. Craddock.

Willis Tillet.
D. Haymen.
Daniel Mann.
Ellis Midgett.

Martin Twiford. John D. Twiford.
James Twiford. Samuel B. Tillet.
T. M. Walker. J. D. Midgett.

NEW BERN, N. C.

E. B. Lane. G. N. Ives.
Thomas Daniels. C. T. Watson.
D. Bell & Co.

OLD TRAP, CAMDEN COUNTY, N. C.

Samuel Leary. Peter Burgess.
Wilson Burgess. W. Burgess.
John K. Jones. Dempsey Wilson.
Caleb Kite. Alexander Needham.
Nathan Kite. John Gray.
Seth Needham. Ben Gregory.

POPLAR BRANCH, CURRITUCK COUNTY, N. C.

Jordan Poynier. John Hampton.
Mace Hampton. Mason Parker.
W. H. Parker. H. B. Crane.
Pat A. Crane. J. Dowdy.
William Simpson. Dey & Wood.

ROCKY HOCK, CHOWAN COUNTY, N. C.

J. D. Parrish.

STUMPY POINT, DARE COUNTY, N. C.

John W. Casey. John H. Wise.
D. P. Gray. B. F. Wise.
M. Troiford. D. B. Midyett.

WASHINGTON, N. C.

D. W. Gaskill.

HOTELS.

To the great, ever-moving army of men and women whose business forces them to travel, or time-killing tourists who travel because they have no business to force them to stay at home, the following list of hotels, which number among the best in their respective cities, can be read with profit:

AURORA, N. C.

"Thompson House," Mrs. W. A. Thompson, Proprietor.

COLUMBIA, TYRRELL COUNTY, N. C.

"Columbia House," W. L. Spruill, Proprietor.

CURRITUCK COURT HOUSE, N. C.

"Sound-Side Hotel," Wilson Walker, Proprietor.
"Granberry Hotel," Geo. W. Granberry, Proprietor.

DURHAM, N. C.

"Hotel Claiborne," A. B. Sites, Proprietor.

EDENTON, N. C.

"Woodward House," J. L. Rogerson, Proprietor.
"Bay View," F. A. White, Proprietor.

ELIZABETH CITY, N. C.

"Albemarle House," Mrs. Wm. Underwood, Proprietor.
"River View Hotel," A. L. Pendelton, Proprietor.

GOLDSBORO, N. C.

"New Arlington," } Will Hunter, Proprietor.
"Gregory House,"

GATESVILLE, N. C.

"Merchants' Hotel" and Livery, D. E. Riddick, Proprietor.
"United States Hotel" and Livery, T. E. Hayes, Proprietor.

HENDERSON, N. C.

"Central Hotel," B. I. Powell, Proprietor.

HERTFORD. N. C.

"Eagle House," W. R. Shannonhouse, Proprietor.

KINSTON, N. C.

"Hotel Tull."
"Nunn's Hotel."

LOUISBURG, N. C.

"Eagle Hotel," C. C. Harris, Proprietor.

MANTEO, DARE COUNTY, N. C.

"Goodwin House," J. E. Goodwin, Proprietor.

NEW BERN, N. C.

"Hotel Albert," M. Patterson & Son, Proprietors.

NEW YORK, N. Y.

"New England Hotel," cor. Bowery and Bayard (for gentlemen only).

NORFOLK, VA.

"St. James," J. A. Kennedy, Proprietor.

PHILADELPHIA, PA.

"Hotel Hilton," Hilt & Schlichter, Proprietors.

PLYMOUTH, N. C.

"Latham House," Mrs. J. W. Latham, Proprietor.

RALEIGH, N. C.

Moseley's American and European House, 126 Fayetteville street.

SWAN QUARTER, HYDE COUNTY, N. C.

"Swindell Hotel," W. B. Swindell, Proprietor.

WASHINGTON, N. C.

"Merchants' Hotel," Main street, Spencer Bros., Proprietors.

WINDSOR, BERTIE COUNTY, N. C.

"American House," J. R. Moody, Proprietor.

WINTON, HERTFORD COUNTY, N. C.

"Winton Hotel," Jordan & Parker, Proprietors.

NORFOLK SUPPLEMENTARY LIST.

The following list embraces all the leading transportation lines of the city of Norfolk and several well-known banking houses, business establishments and offices of professional gentlemen:

Railroads.

Norfolk Southern, M. K. King, General Manager.
Seabord & Roanoke, L. L. Myers, Superintendent.
Norfolk & Western, W. B. Bevil, General Passenger Agent.
Chesapeake & Ohio, H. W. Fuller, General Passenger Agent.
New York, Philadelphia & Norfolk, R. B. Cooke, General Passenger and Freight Agent.
Atlantic & Danville, Chas. B. Peck, General Manager.
Norfolk & Virginia Beach, T. O. Troy, General Manager.
Norfolk & Ocean View.

Steam-ship Lines.

Old Dominion Steam-ship Company, Culpeper & Turner, Agents.
Clyde Line, J. W. McCarrick, General Southern Agent.
Merchants & Miners' Transportation Company, V. D. Groner, General Agent.
Baltimore Steam Packet Company, W. Randall, Agent.
Albemarle & Chesapeake Canal Company, Franklin Weld, President.
North Carolina Lines, C. W. Jester, Agent.
James River Line, J. W. McCarrick, Agent.
Potomac Steam-boat Company, V. D. Groner, Agent.
Norfolk & Fredricksburg Line, Wm. Randall, Agent.
Ronoake, Norfolk & Baltimore Line, Chas. Gurley, Agent.

Suffolk Line, J. W. Perry & Co., Agents.
Roanoke River Line, W. Y. Johnson, General Agent.
Steamer Bonita, Charles Gurley, Agent.
Norfolk & Dismal Swamp Steam-boat Company, Henry Roberts, Superintendent.

Banks.

Bank of Commerce.
Bank of Norfolk.
Burrus Bank.
Home Savings.
Marine.
Norfolk National.

Baker and Confectioner (Wholesale and Retail).

James Reid & Co., 87 Main street.

Box Factory.

W. Tompson Barron.

Dentist.

Dr. A. D. Barrett, 148 Main street.

Detectives.

J. T. James & Co., 109 Main street.

Dry Goods and Notions.

H. R. Anderson & Co., 202 Main street.
Russell & Simcoe, 200 Main street.

Engines and Boilers.

T. A. Perry, Manufacturers' Agent. (See advertisement).

General Commission Merchant.

R. A. Dobie, 2 and 4 Roanoke Square. (See advertisement).

Groceries (Wholesale).

Washington Taylor & Co., 14, 16, 18 Commerce street. (See advertisement).

T. A. Williams & Co., cor. Commerce and Elizabeth streets.

Groceries, Wines and Liquors.

C. W. Morse, 131 Main street.

Iron Works.

"Elizabeth," C. W. Pettit, Proprietor.

Baggage Express.

Jenkins' Norfolk & Portsmouth Express.

Photographer.

J. J. Faber, 21 Bank street. (See advertisement).

Powder (Sporting and Blasting).

Washington Taylor & Co., 14, 16, 18 Commerce street. (See advertisement).

Pork Butcher, Sausage, Head-cheese, &c.

Wm. Proescher, 14 and 16 City Market.

Provisions, Butter, Lard, Cheese, &c.

H. A. Tarrall & Co., 17 and 19 City Market.

Real Estate.

E. C. Lindsey & Co., 124 Main street.

Sale, Livery and Feed Stable.

C. A. Whaley, 79 Union street.
J. B. Brickhouse, 68 Union street.

Tobacco, Cigars and Snuff.

Hamburger Bros., 93 and 95 Water street.

Undertakers.

S. H. Hines & Co., 86 Bank street.
H. C. Smith & Co., 20 Bank street.

NEW BERN SUPPLEMENTARY LIST.

Ice Factory.
George R. Jarman.

Groceries, Wines and Liquors.
James F. Taylor, foot of Middle street.

www.ingramcontent.com/pod-product-compliance
Lightning Source LLC
Chambersburg PA
CBHW020816230426
43666CB00007B/1033